*A New Rationale
for Corporate Social Policy*

Committee for Economic Development
Supplementary Paper Number 31

A New Rationale for CORPORATE SOCIAL POLICY

William J. Baumol
Rensis Likert
Henry C. Wallich and
John J. McGowan

Heath Lexington Books
D.C. Heath and Company
Lexington, Massachusetts

COPYRIGHT © 1970 *by the* Committee for Economic Development.

All rights reserved. No part of this book may be reproduced or utilized in any form or by any means, electronic or mechanical, including photocopying, recording, or by any information storage or retrieval system, without permission in writing from the Committee for Economic Development.

ACKNOWLEDGMENT: The preparation of this book was aided by a grant from the JDR 3rd Fund.

Printed in the U.S.A.
First printing, December, 1970.

COMMITTEE FOR ECONOMIC DEVELOPMENT
477 Madison Avenue, New York, N. Y. 10022
Library of Congress Catalog Card Number 79-148184

A CED SUPPLEMENTARY PAPER

This Supplementary Paper is issued by the Research and Policy Committee of the Committee for Economic Development in conformity with the CED Bylaws (Art. V, Sec. 6), which authorize the publication of a manuscript as a Supplementary Paper if:

a) It is recommended for publication by the Project Director of a subcommittee because in his opinion, it "constitutes an important contribution to the understanding of a problem on which research has been initiated by the Research and Policy Committee" and,

b) It is approved for publication by a majority of an Editorial Board on the ground that it presents "an analysis which is a significant contribution to the understanding of the problem in question."

This Supplementary Paper relates to the Statement on National Policy, *Educating Tomorrow's Managers*, issued by the CED Research and Policy Committee in 1964.

The members of the Editorial Board authorizing publication of this Supplementary Paper are:

E. SHERMAN ADAMS	*Members of the Board of Trustees*
RAYMON H. MULFORD	*of the Committee for Economic Development*
WALTER W. HELLER	*Member, CED Research Advisory Board*
EDWARD S. MASON	*Associate Member, CED Research Advisory Board*
ALFRED C. NEAL	*President of the Committee for Economic Development*
DAVID C. MELNICOFF	*Project Director of the CED Subcommittee on Business Structure and Performance*

This paper has also been read by the Research Advisory Board, the members of which under the CED Bylaws may submit memoranda of comment, reservation, or dissent.

While publication of this Supplementary Paper is authorized by CED's Bylaws, except as noted above its contents have not been approved, disapproved, or acted upon by the Committee for Economic Development, the Board of Trustees, the Research and Policy Committee, the Research Advisory Board, the Research Staff, or any member of any board or committee, or any officer of the Committee for Economic Development.

CED RESEARCH ADVISORY BOARD—1970

Chairman
CHARLES L. SCHULTZE
The Brookings Institution

WILBUR J. COHEN
Dean, School of Education
The University of Michigan

OTTO ECKSTEIN
Department of Economics
Harvard University

WALTER W. HELLER
Department of Economics
University of Minnesota

LAWRENCE C. HOWARD
Dean, Graduate School of Public
 and International Affairs
University of Pittsburgh

CHARLES P. KINDLEBERGER
Department of Economics and
 Social Science
Massachusetts Institute of Technology

JOHN R. MEYER
President
National Bureau of Economic Research, Inc.

FREDERICK C. MOSHER
Woodrow Wilson Department of
 Government and Foreign Affairs
University of Virginia

DON K. PRICE
Dean, John Fitzgerald Kennedy School
 of Government
Harvard University

ELI SHAPIRO
Sylvan C. Coleman Professor
 of Financial Management
Graduate School of Business Administration
Harvard University

MITCHELL SVIRIDOFF
Vice President, Division of National Affairs
The Ford Foundation

PAUL N. YLVISAKER
Professor, Public Affairs and Urban Planning
Woodrow Wilson School of Public and
 International Affairs
Princeton University

Foreword

To what extent can corporate involvement in social problem-solving be justified when such activity lies outside the usual framework of the marketplace?

In addressing themselves to this issue, the authors of these papers suggest that long-range corporate self-interest may be compatible with some types of social "do-goodism." They observe that to one degree or another many corporations are already involved in public-interest activities—or would become involved if an adequate rationale were available. Such a rationale, note Henry C. Wallich and John J. McGowan in their paper, "will be helpful to the extent that management is looking not so much for guidance as to what it ought to do, but for an economic justification of what it already wants to do on compassionate or other grounds."

In these papers, the authors examine various bases for a defense of corporate social involvement, examining the consesequences and implications inherent in each approach to the problem.

William C. Baumol explores the concept of "public goods" as it applies to corporate contributions for philanthropic and similar purposes. Wallich and McGowan show how diversification of ownership can radically alter the "interest of the stockholder," with the result that corporate activities not worthwhile to the stockholder in a single firm become so to the diversified stockholder. Rensis Likert explores the possibilities of human resource accounting as these relate to the value of the loyalty of a corporation's various "publics" — shareholders, bankers, customers, suppliers, communities.

These papers were prepared in the course of CED's on-going deliberations in the general area of corporate leadership and responsibility, which have spanned nearly a decade. Out of these studies have come CED's policy statement on *Educating Tomorrow's Managers* (1964) as well as more recent publications, including a supplementary paper on *Top Management Development and Succession* and a volume of papers on *Business and Social Progress: Views of Two Generations of Business Executives*. The latter publication resulted from a series of informal discussions on the future role of the corporation, sponsored by CED to mark its twenty-fifth anniversary in 1967.

In pursuing its studies in this field, CED's Subcommittee on Business Structure and Performance has found the papers comprising the present volume to be of use in its deliberations. They are published as supplementary papers with the thought that they will also be of interest to a wider audience. It should be emphasized that the ideas expressed in these papers represent solely the individual opinions of the authors and in no way reflect CED's views.

David C. Melnicoff, *Project Director*
First Vice President
Federal Reserve Bank of Philadelphia

Contents

Foreword vii

1. **Enlightened Self-Interest and Corporate Philanthropy** 3
   William J. Baumol

2. **The Influence of Social Research on Corporate Responsibility** 20
   Rensis Likert

3. **Stockholder Interest and the Corporation's Role in Social Policy** 39
   *Henry C. Wallich
   and John J. McGowan*

Notes 61

Contributors 65

Index 67

A New Rationale
for Corporate Social Policy

1. Enlightened Self-Interest and Corporate Philanthropy

William J. Baumol

Giving by corporations is in at least one respect a paradoxical phenomenon. The corporation owes its existence and its continued prosperity to the successful operation of the economy and the viability of the social arrangements. Since a significant segment of the institutions vital for the functioning of that society are financed largely on an eleemosynary basis, it is surely appropriate for the corporations to help to support the operations of these nonprofit groups. Gifts by private firms are justified not merely as a matter of their indebtedness to the nonprofit institutions for their past accomplishments, but also as a matter of self-interest, inasmuch as the deterioration of institutions such as universities and hospitals would no doubt have serious consequences for private enterprise. Yet it is also arguable that the business of the corporation is just business and that philanthropy therefore has no legitimate role in its operations. In this view, the funds in question should be passed on by the corporation to its stockholders, who would then decide for themselves the amounts they wish to give and the groups to which they desire to make their contributions.

It should be emphasized that reservations about the legitimacy of corporate philanthropy are not confined merely to extreme conservatives or to the greediest of stockholders. The intrusion of the business firm into areas of social activity that do not concern it is feared by many of those who consider themselves nineteenth century liberals, as well as by those in the ranks of the more radical. Anyone to whom the "military-industrial complex" is suspect may well view with concern any growth in dependence upon the nation's business firms of its arts and its educational system. Reservations have been expressed about management's power to allocate society's resources among such institutions, management having no public mandate for such an activity nor any obligation of formal responsibility to the general public.

More vociferous, however, are stockholder groups who hold that management has no right to give away funds that legitimately belong to the holders of the company's equity. Pressures from this source have been at least partly responsible for holding average corporate giving to little more than 1 per cent of company pretax profits.[1]

There is a solution to the dilemma posed by such reservations, and it has the sanction of the courts. Corporate giving has been found appropriate so long as it serves the interests of the firm, broadly defined. Surely, the argument runs, a gift to a department of engineering which will help to provide trained personnel to the company in the future is no less appropriate than a payment to a supplier of raw materials for the inputs which he provides to the firm. Neither of these involves an intrusion of management into an area beyond its legitimate concern, and neither is in any sense a giveaway of the stockholders' resources.

Once this argument is accepted it can be stretched considerably. One can maintain, for example, that a company with operations that must unavoidably take place in urban locations has a legitimate reason to invest in the viability of the nation's cities. If our cities cannot survive without better housing and education in the ghettos, then, such a firm must be prepared for its own sake to contribute toward their improvement.

Later in this paper it is shown that even this resolution of the paradox is not without its difficulties. An understanding of the problem is important not simply as a theoretical matter, but as an essential element in the practicalities of corporate philanthropy. Until the problem is understood and the means to deal with it are devised and implemented, there may be no possibility of expanding materially the rate of corporate giving which to many people, both inside and outside corporations, is rather disappointing.

Background of Corporate Contributions

Before World War II, corporate contributions ran considerably below their current levels, both relatively and in absolute terms. During the 1930's giving by the nation's corporations usually amounted to some 0.4 per cent of net profits. The total sum involved ran between $30 million and $40 million. By 1966 philanthropic outlays by corporations had reached some $800 million.

Toward the end of the war, giving for the first time exceeded one per cent of net profits—its approximate current rate. It is plausible that this rather dramatic upsurge can be ascribed largely to the excess profits tax, under whose provisions 95 per cent of marginal company earnings went to the government. At such tax rates giving clearly became very inexpensive to the stockholder, who lost only five dollars for every hundred dollars given away. This observation is significant because it suggests that the magnitude of corporate giving can be influenced significantly by government policy.

However, not all policy measures designed for the purpose are equally effective. There is no evidence, for example, of a corresponding upsurge in the period following the 1935 amendment in the Internal Revenue Code, which permitted for the first time the deduction of charitable contributions by corporations up to a maximum of 5 per cent.[2]

After the end of the war, the rate of corporate giving fell from 0.8 per cent or higher in 1945–46 to a range between 0.6 and 0.8 per cent toward the beginning of the next decade (Table 1). In more recent years, presumably because of increased social concern on the part of corporate management, corporate donations have once again risen to slightly more than 1 per cent of profits or about one-tenth of 1 per cent of gross national product. In absolute dollars they have increased more than twenty-fold from their levels in the 1930's,[3] and have now achieved a significant role in the operations of the nation's nonprofit institutions.

It has been estimated[4] that by the middle of the 1960's, corporations supplied approximately 4 to 5 per cent of total private philanthropy, with 6 to 8 per cent coming from foundations, the remainder being given by individuals, either directly or in the form of bequests. (Bequests constituted 8 to 10 per cent of the total.) Thus, while corporation giving is by no means a negligible factor, it is the smallest of the three major philanthropic sources. Moreover, those engaged in the raising of philanthropic funds feel that there is considerable room for expansion of giving from this source, relative to the potential flow to be derived from other private donors.

The legal status of corporate contributions has not always been as clear as it is today. It has already been noted that tax deductibility of corporate contributions was first instituted in 1935. Since then various court decisions have dealt with the legalities of corporate giving, notably with the legitimacy of philanthropic donations, under the terms of corporate charters, for purposes providing no *direct* benefits to the firms. Perhaps the most noteworthy decision in this area was that in the *A. P. Smith v. Barlow* case of 1953, in which the New Jersey Superior Court affirmed the right of the company to provide funds to Princeton University. In this case, it was arranged for a friendly stockholder to challenge a gift to the university by a manufacturing company located in New Jersey. The decision, favoring

Table 1 **Philanthropic Contributions of Corporations, 1936–1969**

Year[a]	Net Profit[b] (millions)	Contributions (millions)	Contributions as Per Cent of Net Profit
1936–37	$ 7,771	$ 30	0.39%
1938–39	4,131	27	0.65
1940–41	9,348	38	0.41
1942–43	23,389	98	0.42
1944–45	26,454	234	0.88
1946–47	25,399	214	0.84
1948–49	34,588	239	0.69
1950–51	42,831	252	0.59
1952–53	38,735	399	1.03
1954–55	36,721	314	0.86
1956–57	47,412	418	0.88
1958–59	39,224	395	1.01
1959–60	47,655	482	1.01
1960–61	44,499	482	1.08
1961–62	47,034	512	1.09
1962–63	50,842	595	1.17
1963–64	55,737	657	1.18
1964–65	63,059	729	1.16
1965–66	74,741	785	1.05
1966–67	81,089	805	0.99
1967–68	73,250	829	1.05
1968–69	(n.a.)	865[c]	—
1969–70	(n.a.)	900[c]	—

Notes: [a]The income years given here correspond to the accounting periods which are partly on a fiscal year basis and partly on a calendar year basis. For example, the figures for 1936–37 are for the accounting period which either coincided with the calendar year 1936 or ended July 1936 through June 1937.
[b]The profit figures given for the years after 1964 refer to "total receipts less total deductions," which is comparable to "compiled net profit" for earlier years.
[c]Estimates by the American Association of Fund-Raising Counsel, Inc.

Source: U.S. Internal Revenue Service, *Statistics of Income: Corporation Income Tax Returns* (Washington, D.C.: U.S. Government Printing Office, various years).

the university, was subsequently upheld by the State Supreme Court.

The decision was noteworthy on at least two counts. The first was the justification for the donative powers on the ground that the company could not hope to operate effectively in a society that is not functioning well. Second, the decision was important because it based itself on the common law, consequently offering a legal basis for giving to corporations throughout the country. Some sorts of gifts by corporations are now explicitly authorized by law in most states, and national banks are also authorized to make contributions by an amendment to the National Banking Act.

A survey of patterns of giving by 401 corporations conducted in 1968 indicated that nearly 40 per cent of their gifts went to education, while a slightly smaller proportion was devoted to united funds, hospitals, and organizations collecting for health and welfare. About 7 per cent of the total was devoted to civic causes and about 5 per cent to cultural activities, with the remainder going to miscellaneous groups. For complete data, see Table 2.[5]

This pattern of giving fits in well with the doctrine that corporations should provide funds only to causes that serve the firm's interests, broadly conceived. The trebling of corporate contributions in support of education over the decade 1955–65 can be justified on two grounds. First, this improves the quality of life in the communities in which the companies are located. Second, and more important, it is to the educational institutions that business firms look for their supply of trained personnel.

Gifts related to health and welfare can also be rationalized as directly serving the corporate interests. In trying to attract persons of high quality to their employment, business firms find that they must offer candidates a community in which facilities such as hospitals are well run and readily available. The same is true of cultural activities. Increasingly, companies making heavy use of scientists, engineers, programmers, and other tech-

Table 2 The Company Contributions Dollar, 1968

	401 Companies		216 Companies without Foundation		185 Companies with Foundation	
	(thousands)	% of Total	(thousands)	% of Total	(thousands)	% of Total
Health and welfare						
Federated drives: United Funds and the like	$ 57,257	21.74%	$ 28,689	23.61%	$ 28,568	20.14%
National health agencies (not included above)	4,210	1.60	1,867	1.54	2,343	1.65
National welfare agencies (not included above)	4,822	1.83	1,470	1.21	3,352	2.36
Hospitals						
Capital grants	15,210	5.78	8,390	6.91	6,819	4.81
Operating grants	1,564	0.59	495	0.41	1,068	0.75
Other local health and welfare agencies	9,462	3.59	4,029	3.32	5,433	3.83
Capital grants (excluding hospitals)	5,317	2.02	2,606	2.15	2,711	1.91
Total health and welfare	97,842	37.15	47,546	39.13	50,296	35.45
Education						
Higher education						
Scholarships	10,212	3.88	5,204	4.28	5,007	3.53
Fellowships	4,802	1.82	1,452	1.20	3,350	2.36
Research grants (not treated as a business expense)	8,761	3.33	5,963	4.91	2,798	1.97
Capital funds	25,289	9.60	11,871	9.77	13,417	9.46
Direct unrestricted grants	26,948	10.23	11,318	9.32	15,629	11.02
Grants to state, area and national fund-raising groups	5,884	2.23	2,498	2.06	3,386	2.39
Education-related agencies	3,376	1.28	673	0.55	2,702	1.90
Other	11,189	4.25	3,287	2.71	7,902	5.57
Secondary education						
Capital grants	453	0.17	191	0.16	261	0.18
Other	5,294	2.01	3,324	2.74	1,970	1.38
Total education	102,208	38.81	45,787	37.68	56,421	39.77
Culture (cultural centers, performing arts, museums, etc.)						
Operating funds	5,750	2.18	2,916	2.40	2,834	2.00
Capital grants	7,299	2.77	5,142	4.23	2,157	1.52
Total cultural	13,049	4.95	8,058	6.63	4,991	3.52
Civic causes (municipal and community improvement, good government, and the like)						
Total civic	18,946	7.19	7,819	6.44	11,127	7.84
Other						
Religious causes	1,952	0.74	629	0.52	1,323	0.93
Groups devoted solely to economic education	1,388	0.53	549	0.45	838	0.59
Groups in U. S. whose principal objective is aid to other countries	10,738	4.08	4,205	3.46	6,533	4.60
Causes other than above	13,296	5.05	6,570	5.41	6,723	4.74
Total "other"	27,374	10.39	11,953	9.84	15,418	10.87
Dollars not identifiable because donee is unknown	3,968	1.51	342	0.28	3,631	2.56
Grand Total	253,387	100.00	121,505	100.00	141,882	10.000

Source: John H. Watson, III, *Report on Company Contributions for 1968* (New York: National Industrial Conference Board, 1969), p.1, Table 1.

nical personnel have emphasized in their advertising the availability of cultural activities in their communities. The local theatrical group and the symphony orchestra thus have become an asset of marked economic value to certain corporations. Here, then, are clear-cut examples of corporate giving following the patterns of enlightened self-interest sustained by the courts and by what appears to be general good judgment.

Evaluation of Corporate Philanthropic Performance

While the Internal Revenue Code provisions seem to suggest that 5 per cent of net profits is an appropriate standard, corporate giving has so far hardly exceeded one-fifth of this amount.[6] By way of comparison, it may be observed that individual itemized contributions have run as high as 4 per cent of adjusted gross income, while all taxpayers (whether their returns are itemized or not) have been estimated to devote some 2.5 per cent of their adjusted gross income to philanthropy.

Generosity seems to vary inversely with the size of corporations, as can be seen in Table 3. Until recently smaller companies tended to be the most liberal in their giving, but in the past decade an increasing number of medium-sized companies have become relatively open-handed in their contributions policy. This raises some questions about the relative niggardliness of the largest firms. It also is sometimes suggested that national corporations are particularly remiss in this respect. When a local firm is merged into a company that is national or international in its scope, the amount given to local nonprofit institutions typically suffers a sharp decline. However, in over-all terms, the variation in giving patterns between local and national companies has been narrowing, and Watson reports that in 1968 "the record favors the nationals, contradicting all previous NICB [National Industrial Conference Board] surveys."[7]

Whatever view one takes about the generosity of corporations, it is all too clear that the financial needs of nonprofit organizations are growing precipitously. With costs per student in elementary and higher education rising at nearly 7 per cent per year, even before the recent inflationary upsurge, with medical costs and costs in the performing arts increasing at comparable rates, it is hardly surprising that corporations, as well as other donors, are looked to anxiously for increased support. This question naturally arises: What limits the extent of corporate giving to such groups? If corporations provide support to philanthropic activities in response to the donors' own interests —and solely for reasons of self-interest as defined in the previous section—why then is there a scarcity of funds supplied by the nation's business firms?

Self-Interest and Public Goods

To analyze the structure of the problem it is necessary to digress into a subject that may at first appear to be irrelevant —the nature of so-called public goods. Briefly, the point is that while the pursuit of self-interest will assure the supply of adequate amounts of most goods and services in a free enterprise system, there exists an important class of services which econ-

Table 3 **Contributions as a Per Cent of Net Income According to Company Size, 1968**

Company Size by Number of Employees	Number of Companies	Net Income before Taxes (thousands)	Contributions (thousands)	Contributions as Per Cent of Net Income
0–249	7	$ 5,276	$ 170	3.22 %
250–499	15	24,926	400	1.60
500–999	24	88,161	992	1.12
1,000–4,999	106	1,914,013	16,404	.85
5,000–9,999	44	2,084,757	16,486	.79
10,000–24,999	66	6,690,541	43,467	.64
25,000 and over	66	23,465,777	156,460	.66
Total	328	34,273,454	234,381	.68

Note: Insurance companies are not included.
Source: John H. Watson, III, *Report on Company Contributions for 1968* (New York: National Industrial Conference Board, 1969), p. 2, Table 2.

omists refer to as public goods, the supply of which is likely to fall far short of the amount desired by the public. It can be shown that the supply of such goods serves the interests of consumers in exactly the same way as the services of many nonprofit activities serve the interests of corporations. Yet unless special arrangements are made, the activity level in both cases is likely to fall far short of that which is appropriate in terms of the interests of those concerned. The following pages undertake to show precisely how such problems can arise, why they apply in particular to the issue of corporate giving, and what can be done to overcome them.

As already indicated, for a very substantial proportion of the goods and services provided by our economy, the profit system is an adequate device to assure the supply of quantities at least approximately equal to the amounts demanded by consumers. If potential purchasers increase the number of pairs of shoes or shirts that they desire, and are willing to pay for them, the supply will be forthcoming. This is so because the supplier can normally earn a profit if—and only if—he follows the patterns of consumer demand in the manner just described. A critical element in this process, as we will see in a moment, is what economists have labelled "the excludability property" that characterizes such items. If the consumer does not pay for the item, he can be excluded from its use—no payment, no shirt.

There does in fact exist a substantial number of products which do not have the excludability property. Compare the cleaning of an office with the cleaning of the air in a city. The suppliers of the former service can exclude from its benefits anyone who does not pay the fee—if one does not pay, his office is not cleaned. But the suppliers of clean air, that is, the manufacturers of filtering devices, etc., once having purified the atmosphere, cannot prevent any inhabitant or for that matter any visitor, from enjoying the improvement. Clean air is not a salable commodity because once it is supplied to anyone it is automatically available *without payment* to everyone else. The supplier has no way to exclude anyone from using it because of failure to pay a price for it.

This is the fundamental property of all public goods. Its benefits cannot be provided to one purchaser without automatically providing them to many other individuals. In some cases the number of persons benefited will be very large (e.g., in the provision of national defense). In other cases, as in the elimination of air pollution in a single city, a more restricted set of individuals will gain. Sometimes (as in snow removal from a dead-end street) the number of persons benefiting will be very small. But in all these cases once the job is done for one person, it will be accomplished for everyone in the pertinent group.

Consider now the position of an individual in such a group, one whose self-interest will be served by the provision of the service in question. If he were to undertake to contract for the job, he would be providing benefits to the other members of the group; i.e., he would be offering to the group what are called "external benefits". He would be in the position of bearing all of the costs by himself while reaping only a proportion of the benefits, and clearly this may not be a reasonable proposition. While it might well be worth his while if he could arrange to pay his pro rata share of the costs, it may be quite undesirable for him when he has to bear the entire expense himself. Even where the individual does undertake to pay for the service, he will frequently be prepared to undertake far less of it than he would if the group were acting together.

Where such goods are in question, there are two ways in which their supply is usually handled. The first is for the government to supply them and to assign to each of the beneficiaries a share of the cost in the form of taxation. Where the number of individuals affected is relatively large, this may be the only practical way to assure the production of the good or service. That is why such items are called "public goods" and why pollution control and national defense are normally handled by legislation.

A second way of arranging for the supply of public services is typical when the number of persons affected is relatively small. In such circumstance, it is administratively feasible to organize a cooperation group—a consortium. A neighborhood association in a private street may assess each of the—say, ten—resident homeowners one-tenth of the costs of snow removal, and then arrange for the job to be done. The voluntary group works because it is able to "internalize the externalities." The benefits, while in part external to any one individual, are internal to the association. The entire group that benefits is involved in payment of the costs. Taking the group rather than the individual as the relevant decision unit, the excludability property holds as effectively as it does in the sale of a shirt to a single customer.

Practical Application: Oil Exploration

The notions that have been described in the preceding section are not mere abstractions. They are extremely practical in their import; and the growing seriousness of such problems as pollution, road crowding, and urban decay are at least in part manifestations of these relationships.

Similar problems affect the operations of practical businessmen, and in some cases they have at least developed means like those previously discussed in order to deal with them. A particularly clear example is provided by oil exploration. This activity is characterized by fragmentation in the ownership of real estate that is thought to be oil-bearing. If four persons own portions of a field that may contain oil, it is necessary for only one of them to test for its presence. One test boring can suffice to determine for all four property owners whether they should construct their own wells.

However, the individual who undertakes the test boring obviously supplies a public good, because he bears all the cost himself. Whether or not he turns out to have produced a dry hole, the others will have obtained, absolutely free, some extremely valuable information. In such cases the consortium is the obvious way to make sure that such explorations take place and to guarantee that each beneficiary bears a share of the costs. This is apparently the pattern that has emerged. Exploration does in fact take place under the joint sponsorship of those who stand to gain thereby.

However, the industry has not left these matters to chance. It does not rely only on the goodwill of each of the individual property owners to assure the formation of such consortia. The courts are prepared to enforce their formation. Under current arrangements, the owner of such a property need merely propose a set of reasonable offers to the others who stand to benefit. This may involve a cost-sharing agreement which compensates him by a stake in the profits of the other wells, or some other equivalent scheme; and if the courts find the terms to be acceptable the others involved may be required to agree to one of the offers. In this way a quasi-voluntary association principle has been institutionalized as a matter of good business policy, a means to assure that the public good in question is in fact supplied.

Application to Corporate Philanthropy

After this long digression we may return to the basic subject, the volume of corporate philanthropy. We began with the proposition that such funds can normally be expected to flow to activities which serve the enlightened self-interest of the firm. But we have just seen that self-interest may not be enough to assure the supply of a desired service, and that even where some service is supplied, its volume will be less than the amount that is optional from the point of view of the beneficiaries.

The recipients of corporate philanthropy typically bear all of these characteristics. A grant to an educational institution, even if it is restricted—say, to a chemistry department—does not guarantee that the increased supply of chemists will flow exclusively to the donor. More trained individuals will also become available to other companies, including perhaps the direct competitors of the donor firm. Similarly, a gift to a symphony orchestra may make the company's community more attractive to engineers who come to work for it, but it will inevitably help other firms in the area in a similar way. A contribution to an outdoor recreation project which makes the city a safer place for the corporation to operate also simultaneously contributes to the safety of other activities.

Indeed, it is difficult to think of a significant class of beneficiary of corporate philanthropy whose activity cannot be described as the supply of a public good. Nor is this purely accidental. If it were otherwise it would simply be incorrect to describe the company's payment as a gift. If, as an object of company self-interest, the activity could be supplied to our firm all by itself, the activity would have the exclusion characteristic that permits its supply on a profit-making basis by some private enterprise. Nonprofit enterprises do not operate in such fields because there is no need for them.

The consequence is another difficulty that characterizes the supply of all public goods. The company that makes a contribution toward their provision is, strictly speaking, not acting in accord with its own interests. The term "enlightened self-interest" is a euphemism which refers to a combination of factors: the public pressures for a "socially responsible" stance on the part of the firm, the social conscience of management, and its hope that its own contributions will serve as an example to others. Yet as with other public goods, the output of these philanthropic services is likely to be well below what is optimal from the point of view of all companies taken together. Each one of them by itself will finance far less of such activities than it would wish to do if all other enterprises were to undertake to match its contributions.

In this the firm is the victim of what has been described as "the tyranny of the small decision." Each company knows that its own contribution can make little difference to the overall future of higher education. If others fail to contribute, one firm alone cannot save the private universities, while if others do provide sufficient funding, this company's benefaction will not add very much. The net result is that education will not receive as much from industry as it is in the interests of private enterprise as a whole to contribute.

Perhaps the resolution to the dilemma may be found by taking a lesson from other situations involving public goods. The consortium of business donors may go far in dealing with the difficulty. Consider a group of firms which benefit from the presence of a regional theater in their community. If those companies form an association in which each pledges to bear its share of the deficit of the theater, provided all other members also do so, then the connection between the outlay and the return will become a direct one. The externalities will have been internalized. Each management will indeed be able to say to its stockholders that the outlay is a simple matter of economics and self-interest. Moreover, the cost incurred by each will be small, but the effectiveness of its contribution in preserving the activities of the theater will be very substantial. Similarly, consortia may be formed to sustain a private college or a hospital or any other nonprofit enterprise whose welfare is essential for the interests of the group. The initiative for such an association may appropriately come from the contributor corporations or from the organizations they are designed to support. In some cases one might consider utilization of industry or trade organizations that are already in operation—here corporate executives can bring their proposed contribution programs, decide on an appropriate apportionment of the cost, and work out a detailed plan and time schedule.

In any event, this organizational innovation seems well worth trying, for it may succeed in providing a far more direct connection between the firm's contribution and the benefits it receives from the social activity in question. If one is not to be bound by tradition in the area of corporate philanthropy, one must seek for precisely that sort of development—for novel means that can make more immediate the element of self-interest involved in the firm's contribution. Only in this way can stockholders be reassured, and management induced to increase its contributions to a level commensurate with the social returns to the supported activity. The analogy with the provision of other public goods suggests that the consortium of firms, all bound together in the support of one or a set of nonprofit institutions, may prove an effective instrument to provide the enlightenment on the self-interest of the contributor which currently seems in somewhat short supply.

Activities That Can Be Undertaken by Individual Firms

A number of firms have been attempting on their own to systematize and facilitate their contributions programs. The means they have adopted are of some interest as measures that might be considered by others who desire to act on these issues by themselves.

A number of corporations have undertaken to formalize their contribution procedures in a variety of ways. Some have established contribution committees, some have assigned the task of contribution administration and planning to full-time employees, hired specifically for the task. Many firms now have specific budgets devoted exclusively to their program of gifts. A survey conducted in 1963 indicated that 79 per cent of the respondents prepare an annual contributions budget, a 15 per cent increase over the 1956 figure.[8] A somewhat more recent study reported that some 15–20 per cent of the companies surveyed employed a formula determining how much they give.[9]

Perhaps the most important development in this category has been the advent of the company foundation. From a mere twenty such organizations in existence before 1939, their number had grown by 1962 to over 1,500. More than 60 per cent of these were established during World War II and the Korean

War, when tax rates were extraordinarily high. Aside from any tax advantages they may offer, such foundations are useful because they can impart stability to the donation process. By cutting the tie between the volume of philanthropy and the level of current profits, the foundation protects the company from the year-to-year vicissitudes in its earnings.

All of these innovations have obviously facilitated corporate philanthropy. But corporate giving will no doubt be stimulated most effectively by continued managerial reassessment of the firm's stake in the functioning of society. As businessmen see more clearly and are able to show more effectively to their stockholders that the company's prosperity depends on the health of the communities in which it operates, it will become clearer that self-interest is indeed served by corporate contributions. The company pays a high price for operating in a region where education is poor, where living conditions are deplorable, where health is poorly protected, where property is unsafe, and where cultural activity is all but dead. As it grows clear to stockholders and others immediately concerned that these circumstances are all more expensive than corporate giving, the rationality of business philanthropy must become obvious.

It will also be recognized that for business firms this is often a matter which can only be dealt with collectively, by voluntary groupings of firms rather than by the individual enterprises. For it is only such groupings of firms that can provide resources sufficient to make the difference. Groups of firms have long known how to band together when their narrower interests are concerned. In a society where education, health facilities, and social services generally are beset by precipitously mounting costs, the long-range dangers to the business community may be far greater than the threats against which firms have stood together in the past.

2. The Influence of Social Research on Corporate Responsibility

Rensis Likert

For decades there has been a steady increase in the magnitude and variety of governmental controls over business. Whenever any important sector of society suffered what it perceived to be intolerable abuses over a period of time, it sought recourse through political action in the form of governmental controls. When this occurred, the accumulated resentments typically brought about more restrictive restraints than were necessary. Each of these over-corrections usually has deprived business of the flexibility required to conduct its affairs in a constructive, efficient, and adaptive manner.

As our society becomes even more highly industrialized and our technologies more complex, the demand for further governmental controls is likely to grow. For example, the pollution of air and water by industrial waste, which causes health and other human problems, creates demands for new or extended governmental controls. As research enables our nation to increase its productivity and the level of living, it is at the same time creating conditions likely to lead to the demand for greater surveillance of industry by government.

Are there any developments in sight which may in part offset the trend toward more control by government over business? Governmental controls are necessary when intolerable abuses occur and persist. But it is to the advantage of all—business, shareholders, customers, citizens, and the government—to have business itself take steps to prevent the occurrence of abuses and to launch remedial action whenever abuses inadvertently occur. Such a situation will come into being when business organizations, especially large firms, conduct their affairs to a greater extent than at present so that (1) all of the persons affected by the activities of a particular firm will feel that it is behaving in a reasonable and responsible manner, and (2) when this situation does not exist, forces will be created within the firm itself which will lead it, *on its own initiative*, to take the required necessary corrective action.

There appear to be two major contributions emerging from social science research which can help to bring about this development.

First, theories and methodologies are now available to develop the procedures for extending the accounting of a firm's assets for internal management guidance. Accounting procedures can be developed for assets such as:
- The human resources of the firm, namely, the present value of the productive capability of the firm's human organization.
- The value of shareholder loyalty, banker and finance community goodwill, customer loyalty, supplier loyalty, and loyalty in the communities where plants or offices are located.

Second, social science research is providing a more complex and more effective system of management than the prevailing systems. It is based on the principles and practices used by the highest producers, the most successful managers in American business. This science-based management system, which yields higher earnings and better performance than prevailing systems of management, has major characteristics of importance to the problem we are considering. The communication and interaction processes of this more productive man-

agement system enable *every* part of an organization or persons affected by it to do the following:
- Initiate action toward decisions that will best serve the long-range as well as the short-range interests of the corporation. These decisions can include those which are highly innovative as well as those which contribute to cooperation and thereby strengthen the firm.
- Support recommended decisions or bring about modifications of them.
- Exert influence to have decisions accepted for which there is the most widespread and strongest support and for which there is impressive evidence that failure to adopt the decision will have costly consequences for the firm.

Science-based Management Systems

Corporate sensitivity and responsiveness to the reactions of its various publics, and to the effect of these reactions on its immediate and long-term profitability and success, depends on accurate information concerning these reactions and their financial consequences. Unfortunately, these data do not exist today. Virtually every corporation is handicapped by inadequate and often seriously inaccurate information on these matters.

These deficiencies and errors in the information available to guide corporate decisions arise from the omission in financial reports of a sizable proportion of a firm's assets. The magnitude of these neglected assets, over which no accounting surveillance is maintained, can be readily demonstrated by considering a major category, namely, the value of the human organization of the firm.

One approach for demonstrating the magnitude of this asset for any particular firm is to ask its top management the following question: "Assume that tomorrow morning your company has all of its plants, equipment, offices, patents, etc., but no people other than the president, and that he has to start the process of hiring personnel, training them, and building them into the successful organization that your company has today. How much would it cost in terms of your annual payroll to rebuild your organization to its present performance level? Would it be equal to one year's payroll, two years', three years', five years', or what?" The estimates obtained in response to this question vary depending upon the kind of industry of which the firm is a part. Estimates from several thousand managers in widely different industries have ranged from one to twenty times payroll, the most frequent responses being three, four, or five times payroll.

The ratio of payroll to earnings, after taxes, for all enterprises has averaged approximately eight-and-a-half to one in the past few years. From company to company this ratio is commonly found to vary from about two to ten times.

If we treat these figures conservatively, assuming that the cost of rebuilding the human organization of a firm would be equal to roughly three times the firm's payroll and that its payroll is about four times its earnings after taxes, then the human organization is worth about twelve times earnings ($3 \times 4 = 12$). This means that, in an average firm, 8 per cent of the value of its human organization is equal to one year's earnings. This estimate will vary from firm to firm, but for virtually every company the value of its human organization will be found to be many times its current earnings.

Another way to compute the value of a firm's human organization is to look at what companies pay for acquisitions. It is not uncommon to have the value of the physical assets amount to no more than 40 to 60 per cent of the purchase price. In some situations, the physical and financial assets are worth less than 10 per cent of the amount paid for the organization. The prices paid for acquisitions clearly reveal that firms generally have substantial proportions of their assets invested in their human organization, customer loyalty, and similar kinds of goodwill.

A third way of estimating the investment in a firm's human organization and various forms of goodwill is to look at the discrepancy between total value and book value. The total value of a firm, as seen by those who own it, can be estimated by the number of shares outstanding times the price per share. This total value can be computed and related to the shareholder's equity as shown in its annual report. For most firms, the shareholder's equity is a fraction (e.g., from one-sixth to one-half) of its total value which again reveals the sizable investment the firm has in its human organization and goodwill.

No matter what approach is used, the value of a firm's human organization and goodwill represent substantial assets that are not controlled or measured by present-day accounting procedures. This lack of accounting control makes it easy for managers deliberately or unintentionally to show what appears to be earnings by partial liquidation of these resources. The present financial reports, moreover, frequently result in top management rewarding managers for action that alienates one or more of a firm's important publics and affects adversely its long-range financial success. These rewards occur in the form of bonuses and promotions granted by top management to those managers who show impressive earnings in current financial reports. These rewards indeed are warranted when the actual performance is as good as the record shows. Many, however, cannot be justified. For what appears to be impressive earnings by a manager are really an increase in cash achieved from liquidating valuable assets of the firm, usually at a fraction of their true value. This phenomenon can be readily demonstrated by taking the value of the human organization as an example.

As background for this discussion, it is necessary to examine the kind of management system that research is demonstrating yields the highest productivity, the greatest earnings, and the best over-all performance. A large number of studies conducted by the Institute for Social Research[1] as well as research by other investigators[2] reveal that the most productive managers in American business are deviating in important ways from the usual theories of management and from the basic principles upon which the management practices of their own firms are based. The principles and practices used by these most productive managers can be integrated into a coordinated management system, the essential character of which is indicated briefly by the items under System 4 in Figure 1.

When managers at various hierarchical levels in U.S. firms are asked to describe the management system of their own firms, their responses fall largely in the range of System 2 and System 3. Although data are not available from an accurate, probability sample of American corporations, the evidence available indicates that the predominant style of management might be described as System 2½.

When managers are asked to report on their own observations and experience, the results, as would be expected, are quite consistent with quantitative research findings concerning the management system that is most productive and profitable. This is revealed by asking managers the following questions with regard to the items in Figure 1:

1. Please think of the *most* productive department, division, or organization you have known well. Then place the letter "h" on the line under each organizational variable in Figure 1 to show where this organization would fall. Treat each item as a continuous variable from the left extreme of System 1 to the right extreme of System 4.

2. Now that you have completed Figure 1 and described the highest producing department or unit you know well, please think of the *least* productive department, division, or organization you know well. Preferably it should be about the same size as your most productive unit and engaged in the same general kind of work. Then put the letter "l" on the line under each organizational variable in Figure 1 to show where, in the light of your observations,

Figure 1. **Table of Organizational and Performance Characteristics of Different Management Systems**

Organizational variable	System 1	System 2	System 3	System 4
1. Leadership processes used				
a. Extent to which superiors have confidence and trust in subordinates	Have no confidence and trust in subordinates	Have condescending confidence and trust, such as master has to servant	Substantial but not complete confidence and trust. Still wishes to keep control of decisions	Complete confidence and trust in all matters
b. Extent to which downward communications are accepted by subordinates	Viewed with great suspicion	Some accepted and some viewed with suspicion	Often accepted but, if not, may or may not be openly questioned	Generally accepted, but if not, openly and candidly questioned
2. Character of interaction-influence process				
a. Amount and character of interaction	Little interaction and always with fear and distrust	Little interaction and usually with some condescension by superiors; fear and caution by subordinates	Moderate interaction, often with fair amount of confidence and trust	Extensive, friendly interaction with high degree of confidence and trust

b. Amount of co-
operative
teamwork present

None	Relatively little	A moderate amount	Very substantial amount throughout the organization

c. To what extent
are subordinates
involved in
decisions related to
their work?

Not at all	Never involved in decisions; occasionally consulted	Usually are consulted but ordinarily not involved in the decision-making	Are involved fully in all decisions related to their work

d. Are there forces
to accept, resist,
or reject goals?

Goals are overtly accepted but are covertly resisted strongly	Goals are overtly accepted but often covertly resisted to at least a moderate degree	Goals are overtly accepted but at times with some covert resistance	Goals are fully accepted both overtly and covertly

Note: A full description of the four systems contains fifty-one organizational variables.
Source: Rensis Likert, *The Human Organization: Its Management and Value*. Copyright © 1967 by McGraw-Hill, Inc., pp.197–211. Used with permission.

you feel this least productive organization falls on that item. As before, treat each item as a continuous variable from the left extreme of System 1 to the right extreme of System 4.

Many different groups of managers, totaling several thousand persons, have described in this manner the highest- and lowest-producing departments that they know well. Quite consistently, the highest-producing department is seen as toward the right end of the table, the lowest-producing department falls to the left. This pattern is, of course, consistent with the substantial research findings previously mentioned upon which System 4 is based.

In the light of this pattern, a very significant finding emerges when experienced managers are asked the following:

> In your experience, what happens in a company when the chief executive officer becomes concerned about earnings and takes steps to cut costs, increase productivity, and improve profits? Does top management usually continue to use the management system it has been employing or does it shift the firm's operation to a management system more toward System 1 or more toward System 4?

Managers overwhelmingly report that when top management seeks to reduce costs, it "tightens up" and shifts its system more toward System 1; i.e., toward a system which managers report from their own observations and experience yields poorer productivity and higher costs, on the average and over the long run, than does the management system in current use by the company.

What are the inadequacies in accounting methods and in financial reports that lead managers and boards of directors to believe that the increased productivity and cash balance yielded by the usual cost reduction efforts represent an increase in earnings when the actual facts are to the contrary?

The usual kinds of cost reduction efforts involve such steps as budget tightening, personnel limitations, the introduction or spread of measured work and of standards, increased pressure to perform at the level of work specified by the standards, etc. All of these steps result in increased hierarchical pressure on the organization and involve a shift upward in the levels where decisions are made in the firm. They represent, as was noted previously, a move toward System 1 management. (It is perfectly feasible, of course, to reduce costs by applying System 4; at present, however, this approach is not commonly used.)

This shift in management style may yield a 25 per cent or even 50 per cent increase in what is reported as "earnings" under current practice, but it yields many unfavorable and costly changes in the human organization that often are not recognized as stemming from this action. It produces less favorable and less cooperative attitudes, greater fear and distrust, more "yessing" of the boss, poorer communication, lowered performance goals, and greater restriction of production. It also results in increased turnover. This turnover occurs most often among the more able and valuable employees since they are the employees who, when disaffection occurs, most readily obtain outside employment offers. Labor relations worsen, grievances increase, and work stoppages become more of a problem after a year or two. These and related developments occur when the usual approach to cost reduction is used. All of them reflect a *decrease* in the value of the human organization.

To produce, say, a 5 to 10 per cent decrement in the value of a firm's human organization and its productive capability, does not take much loss in confidence and trust; poorer communication; worsened motivation; less concern for quality and scrap loss; greater restriction of production; increased turnover among the better engineers, managers, scientists, and trained workers; and worsened labor relations. Since, as we have seen previously, the human organization of a firm can be worth many times its annual earnings (e.g., by a multiple of ten to twenty), a 5 per cent decrease in the value of the human organization in a firm with a return of only fifty cents on each dollar of value would be equal to 25 per cent or 50 per cent of earnings.

A decrease of 5 per cent or 10 per cent or even of 20 per cent in the value of a firm's human organization usually goes unrecognized for some time. Most firms have no quantitative measurements to reveal this decrement. Moreover, it is frequently obscured by changes in products and technological changes. Years later, however, this decrement may be revealed in worsened labor relations or in loss of the firm's share of its market. The true cause of such developments, however, is not generally recognized at the time the decrease occurs.

The preceding analysis sheds light on the reasons why firms, when they wish to increase current earnings, quite generally use cost-reduction programs which involve a shift toward System 1. This shift to a less-effective management system, which actually yields lowered earnings, provides a rapid increase in cash that is reported as "earnings" in the balance sheet. These earnings are not true earnings at all; they are an increase in cash derived from a liquidation of the firm's human resources. This is an expensive way to increase a firm's cash position since damage to a firm's human organization adversely affects its capacity to succeed in the future. The human organization of a firm is its most important asset—the one which is most difficult to replace.

It is equally true, of course, that a firm can as readily increase its cash by liquidating customer loyalty. This is done when it sells shoddy merchandise or provides poor service at the usual price. The goodwill of customer, shareholder, supplier, and community can all be liquidated for current cash, but such liquidation does not represent earnings even though present accounting practices treat the income as such.

The liquidation of the human organization of a firm and of the various forms of goodwill are all accompanied by an unintended effect that is central to the topic of this paper. *They all yield an unfavorable shift in attitudes toward the firm among the publics affected.* An increase in available cash—falsely labelled "earnings"—can indeed be achieved through exploiting one or more of a firm's publics. But this is done at the risk of contributing to resentments, and when the magnitudes of these are great enough, they explode in demands for governmental restraints or controls.

As mentioned previously, the theory and methodology are now available for developing the procedures for human resource accounting. A substantial program of research is under way at the Institute for Social Research to develop the procedures for estimating the present dollar value of the productive capability of a firm's human organization and for measuring changes from period to period in the magnitude of this asset. This work is employing several different approaches to the problem. The first use of human resource accounting in a firm started on a pilot basis on January 1, 1968 in the R. G. Barry Corporation.[3] The 1969 annual report of this firm was the first time the annual report of any firm included estimates of human resources. Work is also under way using methodology now available to test and refine procedures for assigning dollar estimates to the current value and changes in the value of customer loyalty and to the good will of shareholders, bankers, suppliers, communities, and all the other publics important to a firm.

Pending the development of methods for assigning dollar estimates to the value of the human organization of a firm and to its other goodwill assets, quantitative surveillance over them can be maintained. Methods now existing enable a firm to determine whether there has been an increase or decrease in the value of any of these assets. Though these methods do not as yet permit the firm to attach any dollar estimate to such changes, they do reveal the presence and magnitude of any change.

After several years' time, when human resource accounting begins to become operational, the appreciable increase in the accuracy of the information that firms will have then concerning their financial condition will be likely to lead to sounder policies and decisions. These decisions will also be more likely to serve better the interests of the firm's various publics, including its own employees, and lead to less clamoring for governmental controls than might be the case if this more accurate and extensive information were not available.

Reinforcing More Accurate Facts With Better Decision Making

The coordinated system of management designated as System 4, which we examined earlier in this paper, displays characteristics highly relevant to the topic that we are discussing. Several studies employing sophisticated quantitative research methods are beginning to reveal that with this system of management the human organization of the firm is much more tightly knit than is the case with other management systems. Communications flow more readily in all directions, downward, upward, and laterally, without overloading the communication channels. Also, they are more accurate and are accepted with greater confidence. Moreover, in comparison with other management systems, there is substantially greater capacity to foster the high levels of motivation that achieve the organization's goals in an efficient manner. Wasteful conflict is minimized; effective cooperation is attained. There is appreciably better coordination focused on getting the job done in a System 4 organization than in others.

System 4 organizations have an important characteristic that is crucial to their capacity to achieve more effective coordination than occurs with other systems of management. A number of studies[4] have shown that the more nearly a firm's management system approaches System 4 in its decision making and operations, the greater is the capacity of all hierarchical levels of the organization to exert influence on all of the decisions and actions that are taken.

This capacity of lower echelons in an organization to exert influence on what goes on, however, is *not obtained at the expense of the capacity of higher echelons to exercise influence.* Consistently, in study after study, the research findings reveal that the contrary is actually the case. *Each* level in a System 4 organization—top managers, middle-level managers, and the rank and file—can exert appreciably more influence than is possible in other management systems. Equally important is that each, in turn, is more subject to being influenced by each of the other levels. In contrast to other systems, there is a greater *total* capacity in System 4 firms to exert influence, the coordination processes of System 4 being appreciably more effective than those of Systems 1 to 3.

Over the next several years, as firms shift to science-based management systems such as System 4 in order to remain competitive, the communication and influence processes of corporations will enable each of its segments to press for decisions that it feels consider adequately the particular needs and problems of concern to that unit. As a consequence, the needs and desires of the members of a firm and of all those persons served by it or affected by it will have efficient communication channels through which influence on policy and operating decisions can be exercised. The sales department, aware of the needs and wishes of customers, will be able to be heard fully on their behalf. The purchasing department, because of its awareness of the need for dependable and competent sources of supply and the problems that suppliers are facing, will be able to speak for them. The treasurer and fiscal officers will be concerned that the interests of capital sources are adequately considered. Influence exerted upward through the line organization, as well as from the personnel department and from unions, will see that the well-being of the members of the firm are given full consideration. These groups also will speak in behalf of the best interests of the communities in which the firm has plants or offices. Finally, the senior officers and board will represent the shareholders and seek policies and decisions that are in the best long-range interests of the firm and its financial health.

All of these competing and often conflicting demands, from all parts of the firm and from all persons served or affected by it, will flow through the interaction and influence processes of the firm. An essential activity of top management and the board of directors as the central core of these interaction and influence processes will be *to establish corporate objectives* that represent an optimum integration of all of the competing needs and demands. Again in contrast with other management systems, the decision-making processes of System 4 are such that there is *a greater probability that constructive, widely acceptable solutions and objectives will be established.* Because System 4 decision making is characterized less by "win-lose" battling to unsatisfactory outcomes than are other management systems, it is able more often to achieve innovative and integrative problem solving that reaches mutually acceptable solutions.

In previous writings, the author has illustrated this characteristic of System 4 by contrasting it with System 2:[5]

> Problems handled in a System 2, man-to-man interaction pattern are frequently problems of the subordinate and his unit. This is particularly true of problems raised by the lower echelon. The subordinate (*d* in Figure 2) presents his problems to his superior and tries to have them solved from the standpoint of what is best for him and for his unit. The focus of subordinate *d* is to obtain a decision which facilitates effective performance by his unit, even though the decision may be costly to the total organization. If, for example, *d* heads a production operation, he may be seeking approval for a product change which simplifies the manufacturing operation and thereby reduces his costs. He may seek this action even though the product is less acceptable to consumers and hence harder and more expensive for the marketing department to sell and less profitable to the company.

Figure 2. **Comparison of Management Systems**

Problem-solving Focus in the Man-to-man Model
of Interaction and Decision Making (System 2).

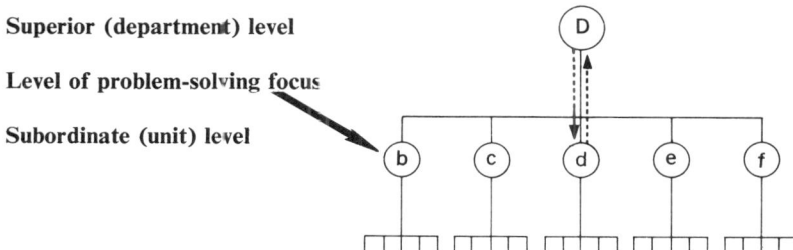

With System 2, man-to-man (D-to-d) decision-making problems, especially those raised by subordinates, tend to be stated, examined, and solved from the point of view of subordinate level; i.e., they serve the interest of the smaller organizational entity at the expense of the well-being of the total organization.

Problem-solving Focus in the Group Model
of Decision Making (System 4).

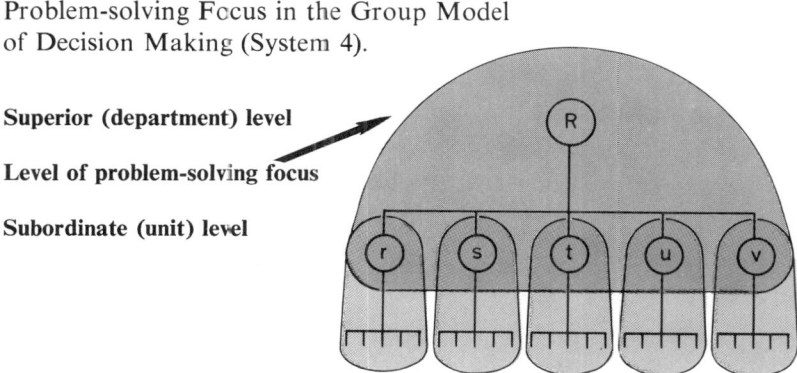

With System 4, problems which affect the subordinate (unit) level only are referred to that level for decision; problems which affect more than one unit are stated as department-wide problems and solved in terms of what is best for the entire department rather than serving the interests of a particular subordinate unit.

Source: Rensis Likert, *The Human Organization: Its Management and Value.* Copyright © 1967 by McGraw-Hill, Inc, pp. 181–182. Used with permission.

In this situation, the superior (D in Figure 2) is handicapped in any attempt to deal with the problem from a broader point of view by the orientation constantly maintained by the subordinate. The superior is also at a disadvantage because often he does not possess all the facts, information, and technical knowledge which his subordinates (*b, c, d, e,* and *f* in Figure 2) have and which are necessary in order to arrive at a solution satisfactory, or at least not detrimental, to the other units affected by the solution (under *b, c, e,* and *f* in Figure 2). There are, consequently, forces present in the decision-making processes of System 2 which tend to encourage the statement and solution of problems focused on what is best for a particular subordinate unit, without proper consideration of the aspects of the problem important to the other units at the same echelon, as well as to the organization as a whole.

When decisions are made by groups which use effective group decision-making methods, as in System 4, they are made with a broader orientation. Any problem raised for consideration tends to be a problem at the *level of the superior* and tends to deal with the needs and requirements of that level (department head R in Figure 2). If a unit head (e.g., *r* in Figure 2) in raising a problem for consideration states it solely from the standpoint of his unit, one of two developments occurs: (1) the superior R, or others in the work group, point out that if the problem deals only with the subordinate unit, that unit should handle it and not raise it for consideration by the superior unit, or (2) the problem is restated by the superior R, or other group members, so that it deals with matters of concern to other units as well as to the one which raised it; i.e., the problem is broadened so that it becomes of department-wide concern. In solving this department problem, the heads of the various units (*r, s, t, u,* and *v*) add the situational requirements, (i.e., the hard facts of life) which they face and which a solution must meet to be acceptable. The solution which emerges from such group decision making is one which is deemed *best for the entire department and for all of its units*. It is not a decision which meets the requirements of one particular unit (i.e., the unit of r in Figure 2) while handicapping the other units (those under s, t, u, and v).

This difference between System 2 and System 4 occurs at every hierarchical level in the organization. There is, consequently, a multiplying effect of the tendency in System 2 organizations to state problems and solve them in terms of what is best for the subordinate level and in System 4 to deal with and solve problems in terms of what is best for the superior level. As a consequence, with System 4, the decisions and actions which emerge are more likely than with System 2 to be those best for the entire organization.

As firms shift to science-based systems of management, such as System 4, their communication, influence, coordination, and decision-making processes will become more efficient than at present. As this shift occurs, each firm will do a better job of establishing objectives which represent an optimum integration of all of the conflicting needs and demands coming to it from its *various* publics. As this occurs, the objectives of the enterprise, its policies, and its specific goals will be more likely than at present to yield results satisfactory to all concerned. Favorable rather than unfavorable attitudes will be established among the firm's various publics.

The Combined Impact of the Two Contributions

The two major contributions emerging from social science research—more accurate financial information and a more effective and more responsive management system—are likely to yield developments which will increase the probability that business will satisfy the felt needs and desires of its various publics. Their combined impact, however, will be appreciably greater than either alone. As human resource accounting comes into use, far more extensive and accurate financial information will become available. All this new information has an important characteristic. It all deals with the reactions of people involved in the organization or affected by it. The new data will reveal the dollar value of their favorable attitudes and continued support. These data will make unequivocally clear the costly consequences to the firm of such short-range kinds of actions as the typical cost-reduction programs previously discussed. When firms have accurate facts available about costs and consequences, sound decisions generally emerge.

The more effective interaction and decision-making processes of System 4 will increase significantly the likelihood that the more accurate financial and other facts yielded by human resource accounting will result in sounder long-range decisions. In turn, the goodwill of all of the relevant publics will be maintained or strengthened. Among all firms which wish to succeed and stay in business, consequently, there will be a decrease in those policies and actions which lead to hostile and resentful reactions and which, in turn, bring about political pressure for governmental controls.

3. Stockholder Interest and the Corporation's Role in Social Policy

Henry C. Wallich and John J. McGowan

Many corporate managements have evinced considerable interest in the social problems that have come to the foreground. A significant school of thought holds that private business should involve itself in these problems. However, the proponents of this view must meet the test of demonstrating that this activity is consistent with stockholder interest. Unless they can show this, they will find it difficult to controvert the opposing case which maintains that management should limit itself to the efficient conduct of the business in the interest of the stockholder.

In this paper, we attempt to show how diversification of ownership radically alters the "interest of the stockholder." Corporate activities become worthwhile to the diversified stockholder that would not be so to the stockholder in a single firm.

This demonstration, laborious and intricate in detail, will be helpful to the extent that management is looking not so much for guidance as to what it ought to do, but for an economic justification of what it already wants to do on compassionate and other grounds. The economic interests analyzed in this paper are perfectly real. If their implementation were to be left solely to market forces, however, the process might be a long and incomplete one. Moreover, these interests are likely to prevail only if markets are "good" and if managements are highly sensitive to the new kind of stockholder interest that is emerging. Hence, the market process can be given an invigorating push by socially-oriented management.

The situation can be compared broadly with that prevailing prior to the 1953 court decision in the *A. P. Smith v. Barlow* case, which gave formal legitimacy to the practice of corporate giving to institutions of higher learning. Many firms that had wished to make such grants, but which had been restrained by legal uncertainties, became free to act.

Today a large number of firms might be prepared to undertake a variety of socially oriented expenditures if they could reconcile them with stockholder interest. This paper makes an effort to provide a reconciliation. Of necessity, the argument must be theoretical. Without strong theoretical underpinnings, any defense of corporate social involvement is likely to remain vulnerable. But the usefulness of the argument does not depend on whether and how soon existing markets, left to themselves, would produce the reactions described. The motive power is expected to come not from market forces, but from an existing desire of many managements to undertake these activities.

What is needed is a release mechanism. If it can be demonstrated that "good" (i.e., highly competitive) markets would in the long run bring about social involvement of corporations, this must be viewed as justifying more deliberate action to bring about involvement more rapidly. It can be viewed also as justifying a certain amount of cooperation among firms, since the results of this cooperation are those that would be produced by a competitive market in the long run. With this paper we seek to contribute to this justification.

Three Degrees of Appropriable Returns

Social policy would be unnecessary if every use of resources that was worthwhile from the point of view of society was also profitable from the point of view of business. If business firms could appropriate (i.e., fully recapture) the marginal value of the benefits they generate, every good and every service would be produced in the amounts that yielded the highest level of welfare for society. It is a familiar fact that many activities yield marginal returns that cannot be recaptured by producers. For example, firms that invest in the training of workers glean returns in terms of higher productivity so long as the workers remain employed by the firm which trained them. When these employees are hired by a competitor, the benefits of higher productivity accrue to him. This investment in manpower training has still been worthwhile for the industry as a whole, but not for the individual firm. Pollution abatement presents an even greater problem. In this case, the benefits accrue largely not only outside the investing firm, but also outside the business sector, although from the viewpoint of society as a whole they may be worth what they cost. These circumstances lead firms to invest less in manpower training, pollution abatement, and other socially desirable activities than their return to society would justify.

Activities such as these can be described as having imperfectly appropriable returns. This means simply that the marginal benefits from these activities, as measured by their impact on the profits of firms engaging in them, undervalue the marginal benefits to society. Two kinds of activities with imperfectly appropriable returns can be distinguished.

First, there are activities whose benefits, even though imperfectly appropriable by the firm undertaking them, are nevertheless completely captured by firms as a group. That is, while the impact on profits of the performing firm undervalues total marginal benefit, the impact on profits of all firms taken together is an accurate measurement of their marginal benefit to society. Such activities can be said to have returns appropriable by the corporate sector.

Second, there are activities whose marginal benefit is

undervalued even when their impact on the profits of firms as a group is considered. Such activities can be described as having returns not appropriable by the corporate sector.

Economic theory seems to provide a clear prescription for corporate behavior in this regard. The function of corporate management is assumed to be the formulation and execution of policies that will lead to maximum stockholder welfare. Stockholder welfare is assumed to be maximized when the market value of the firm is maximized. A policy of including returns not appropriable by a corporation in its evaluation of investment opportunities would lead it to adopt an investment program that would result in lower profits; this in turn would result in a lower market value of the corporation than adherence to a policy of considering only appropriable returns. Consequently, only a policy of considering returns appropriable by the firm contemplating investment is consistent with the stockholders' interest.

By such an argument the dictum is established that substantial corporate involvement in social policy is contrary to the interests of stockholders—a view reexamined here in light of the prevalent tendency for investors to hold diversified equity portfolios. Stated another way, the purpose is to inquire into the proper basis for the evaluation of returns from investment by corporations whose stockholders hold shares in several corporations.

Profit maximization is not, of course, the sole possible rule of corporate behavior. Maximization of present worth is another possibility, but this is a refinement of the profit-maximization rule, not an alternative to it. One alternative explanation of corporate behavior is that corporations set their goals below the maximum, at a level that satisfies the parties concerned; thus the goals they are seeking are not only the profits of the stockholder, but the objectives of the various constituencies with which business deals. The discussion here can abstract from that possibility for one obvious reason. Insofar as corporations have goals other than maximum profits, they are likely to be concerned, among other things, about their social responsibilities. The apparent conflict between stockholder interest and involvement in social policy therefore is of relatively little interest to them. For that very reason we focus on profit-maximizing corporations; not only is this the usual case assumed in economic analysis, but also it is the approach least hospitable to the social involvement of business firms.

It is possible to identify three possible investment bases that a corporation might adopt. The *narrowest* base would take account only of returns directly appropriable by the corporation —the conventional approach to the evaluation of returns. An *intermediate* policy would include returns appropriable through the market system by the corporate sector as a whole. Finally, a *wide-based* approach to evaluation of returns would include not only market-appropriable returns but also returns accruing to the community (including corporations and stockholders) not appropriable through the market by the corporate sector.

Implications of Portfolio Diversification

The theory of portfolio choice explicitly recognizes the uncertainty of returns to equity investment and assumes that stockholder welfare depends upon both expected return and the riskiness of investment alternative. In particular, interest centers on investors who are averse to risk, which means they are willing to accept additional risk only if it is accompanied by higher expected returns. Thus diversification of equity holdings is seen to arise because risk-averse investors, by combining equities, can produce portfolios whose risk and return characteristics allow them to reach a higher return for a given level of risk, or a lower risk for a given return, than they could by holding all their wealth in a single asset.

One implication of these theories of portfolio choice is that, under certain rather restrictive assumptions, there exists a unique, optimal equity portfolio for risk-averse investors that includes all available equities.* This implausible but greatly simplifying case is used to clarify the principle in order to apply it later to more realistic conditions. In the extreme case envisaged here, every investor who chose to hold any of his wealth in equities would hold shares in every corporation, and all such investors would distribute the fraction of their wealth devoted to equities over the existing securities in the same proportion. The resulting situation is perfectly analogous to a situation in which investors were allowed to hold only shares in a mutual fund that in turn owned all the stock of all corporations.

It is immediately clear that under such conditions it would be contrary to the stockholders' interest for individual corporations to adopt the narrow-based approach—that which instructs each corporation to look only at returns appropriable by it and which is the keystone of arguments advocating a minor role in social policy for corporations. If there are investment opportunities which would lead to improved environmental conditions, a better labor force, or whatever, and the returns appropriable by the corporate sector as a whole exceed costs, then they should be seized. Not to seize them deprives investors of returns they might otherwise enjoy. That is, corporations as a group (and singly as well, under reasonable assumptions) will earn more on their invested capital, and stockholders will be better off if these policies are adopted. But corporations will be led to exploit such opportunities only if they adopt, at a minimum, the intermediate-based approach to evaluation of returns —that which includes all returns appropriable by the corporate sector. Therefore, stockholders should desire that all corporations go at least as far as adoption of the intermediate-based approach.

Since adoption of this approach to evaluation of returns

---

*The required assumptions are: (1) the absence of transactions and informative costs; (2) no pair of equities exhibits perfect positive correlation of returns; (3) there is some riskless asset which pays a fixed return; and (4) all investors can borrow and lend at a rate equal to that fixed return.

to investment would lead firms to invest more heavily in activities that social policy aims to promote, such firms might be referred to as socially-minded firms. Corporations not adopting this approach would benefit from the expenditures made by the socially-minded firms without incurring social involvement costs themselves. These mavericks would therefore tend to have higher returns on their investment than those adopting the intermediate-based approach. This disparity in returns might be expected to lead investors to bid for maverick stocks. This in turn would drive up the market value of maverick stocks until the risk-and-return combination offered by these stocks had ceased to offer superior attractions. In effect, therefore, stockholders would not move away from their position of complete diversification.

Maverick corporations, however, would enjoy a lower cost of capital, thanks to the appreciation of their stock. In the very long run, they might outcompete all other corporations. The existence of mavericks, therefore, at the theoretical and probably also at the realistic level, is an impediment to the adoption of the intermediate-based approach here considered.

Two mechanisms, however, will work against maverick propensities and will tend to induce all corporations to adopt the intermediate, if not the widely-based, approach to social involvement. First, social expenditures may be subject, like many other forms of business activity, to increasing costs. In that case it will be in the interests of stockholders to spread social expenditures evenly over all firms, to the point where marginal cost equals marginal appropriable benefit. Under these idealized conditions, self-interest rather than social pressure will weed out the mavericks. Second, if rising costs in social involvement do not prevail, stockholders would nevertheless have a motive to distribute these expenditures evenly. Unless they do, the mavericks may eventually outcompete the socially-involved corporations. This would reduce social expenditures and therefore reduce stockholders' gains from equity ownership.

Effects of the Broad-based Approach

It is thus consistent with stockholder interest for corporations to be socially minded, at least to the extent of including all returns appropriable by the corporate sector through the market system in evaluating investment opportunities. However, the question remains whether an even broader approach is in the interests of the stockholders. In other words, how would stockholders' welfare be affected by adoption of the practice of including returns not appropriable through the market in evaluating investment opportunities?

The answer to this question is clear-cut as long as the assumption that stockholders' welfare depends solely upon the risk and expected return of their wealth portfolios is maintained. Adoption of the broad-based approach will always mean a decrease in returns for corporations, because it implies investing in projects so long as the sum of market appropriable and nonmarket appropriable returns is greater than cost, even though the returns appropriable by the investing corporation are less than its costs. Under the present assumption, stockholders derive no satisfaction from nonmarket returns, hence adoption of the broad-based approach leads them to a lower welfare position and is *a fortiori* contrary to their interests.

Were corporate managers as a group to adopt the broad approach contrary to their stockholders' interest, stockholders would attempt to reduce the proportion of their wealth held in equities. This would lead to a fall in equity prices, capital losses for stockholders, and a rise in the cost of capital for all corporations. The result of this change, it is interesting to note, would not only be a lower stock of physical capital than would otherwise have prevailed. The composition of the stock of physical capital would also be different, because the smaller stock would have been selected by different criteria, namely, on the basis of its social return rather than its private return.

Alternatively, if it is assumed—as is surely likely—that stockholders also derive satisfaction from other things in addition to the risk and return of their wealth portfolios, then the investment opportunities exploited by their corporations may generate benefits for them quite apart from the contribution of those investments to the expected return on equity portfolios. Such benefits may arise because the actions taken by corporations directly affect stockholder welfare. This would be the case when the quality of the environment is improved through cleaner air and water, for example, or more esthetically pleasing structures. It would also be the case when corporate policies contribute to social stability by helping to achieve equality of opportunity, or by helping to right social and economic inequities in other ways. In addition, stockholders may derive indirect benefits from the policies followed by their corporations because the stockholders as individuals are compassionate and share vicariously in benefits directly received by other individuals. Thus, individual stockholders need not necessarily have their own environment improved by the policies of their corporations in order to benefit from those policies. The mere fact that someone benefits from the policies may give satisfaction to some stockholders.

Although stockholders may thus derive satisfaction from nonmarket returns, it does not follow that adoption of a broad-based approach to investment evaluation is necessarily consistent with maximization of their welfare. As discussed above, adoption of such a policy will lead to lower expected monetary returns to the holding of equities. The fall in returns is a measure of the net opportunity cost of adoption of the policy, and those costs are borne by stockholders in accordance with the proportion of outstanding equities which they hold. This means, within the model under discussion, that the expected opportunity costs of following the broad-based approach are borne by stockholders in proportion to their wealth—those with larger equity portfolios pay more. But in contrast to returns appropriable through the corporate sector, the nonmarket returns are not distributed amongst stockholders in proportion to the magnitude of their wealth. Rather, the expected nonmarket returns may be equally or, more likely, randomly distributed over holders of equities.

The problem usually arising when benefits are distributed independently of costs is that each individual maximizes his own welfare by minimizing his contribution to the cost of producing the benefits. In the present context this seems to imply that any investor would prefer those corporations whose stock he holds not to adopt the broad-based approach even when he expected to benefit from its adoption. An alternative statement of this apparent implication is that stockholders would attempt to reduce their holdings in a corporation that adopted the broad-based approach even though they derived net benefits from its adoption.

In the present model, however, which assumes each stockholder to have an interest in all corporations, neither of these forms of behavior is rational for a stockholder who expects to derive net benefits from the adoption of the broad-based approach. If he were to direct his corporations to eschew that policy and if they followed his instruction, there would be no nonmarket benefits produced; he would then be worse off than if they were produced. Consequently, an investor has no incentive to conceal his true preferences with respect to the adoption of a broad-based approach to evaluation of investment opportunities. Nor does he have any reason to prefer some corporations to adopt the policy and some not, since he holds stocks in all of them. Thus, he either prefers all corporations to adopt the broad-based approach or prefers that none of them does.

The answer to the question of whether adoption of the broad-based approach is in the interest of an individual stockholder thus depends solely on the net benefits he receives and how he evaluates them. We can therefore proceed to assess the effects of adoption of the broad-based approach on stockholder welfare under various assumptions about the distribution of wealth and stockholders' preferences.

If wealth were distributed equally and if all investors had identical preferences, adoption of the broad-based approach would be unambiguously in the stockholders' interest, provided nonmarket returns tended to be randomly distributed. Every stockholder would then have the same expectation of nonmarket returns; and because they all are assumed to have identical preferences, they would all value these returns identically. Furthermore, equality of wealth and identity of preferences would insure that all investors had identical portfolios, which in turn would ensure that the cost of nonmarket returns in terms of foregone market returns was equal for all investors. Adoption of a policy of including nonmarket returns in evaluating investment opportunities, and proceeding with those projects whose cost was less than the sum of market and nonmarket returns to stockholders, would lead to higher welfare for every stockholder; only by adopting such a policy would stockholder welfare be maximized.

Inequality in the distribution of wealth and differences in investors' preferences open the possibility that adoption of a broad-based approach would be viewed as an undesirable policy by some and a desirable one by others. In such circumstances it becomes meaningless to inquire whether adoption of the broad-based approach is in the stockholders' interest since they do not speak with a single voice. All that can be done is to trace the consequences of adopting the approach in terms of the effect on stockholder welfare and behavior and on the cost of capital for adopting firms.

Adoption of the broad-based approach by all corporations, when there are stockholders who feel they will thereby be made worse off, has effects qualitatively similar but quantitatively less important than in the case where corporations adopt the broad-based approach while their stockholders derive no satisfaction from nonmarket returns. That is, the attempt by dissatisfied stockholders to shift their portfolios toward nonequity securities would tend to raise the cost of capital for all corporations but leave them on an equal footing relative to each other. Similarly, individual corporations that adopted the broad-based approach would run the risk of offending some stockholders and of incurring a consequent adverse effect on their cost of capital.

It is impossible to say just how great the effect on the cost of capital would be. But the expected decrease in market returns for a corporation attendant upon its adoption of the broad-based approach would be unlikely to cause the price of its securities to fall to the point where the financial rate of return on those securities prevailing prior to the adoption of the broad-based approach—and still prevailing for other stocks—was restored. The higher the share of the firm's stock that was held by dissatisfied investors, the larger the actual price drop. It would also be larger the more closely correlated the returns on this corporation's stock with the returns on other stocks. Highly correlated stocks, such as stocks in the same industry, are good substitutes for each other, and their returns cannot differ very much.

The Realistic Assumption: Limited Diversification

It is helpful at this point to summarize the conclusions that have been reached for the case where risk aversion leads investors to hold the stocks of all firms in their equity portfolios.

First, maximization of stockholder welfare requires firms at a minimum to adopt the practice of including all returns that are appropriable by the corporate sector in evaluating investment opportunities. Adoption of this practice would lead corporations to assume a substantial role in social policy and arguments that corporations should eschew such a role in the interests of stockholder welfare are not applicable in this situation.

Second, there is no general answer to the question of whether the adoption of an even broader-based approach to the determination of returns—one which included returns not appropriable through the market as well as appropriable returns—is in the stockholders' interest. Even if it is assumed that investors derive satisfaction from nonmarket returns, adoption of the broad-based approach is unambiguously consistent with maximization of stockholder welfare only when there is perfect equality of the distribution of wealth and all investors have identical preferences. In other cases it is impossible to say whether adoption of the broad-based approach is in the stockholders' interest. Indeed, it is unrewarding even to address that question, for some stockholders may view favorably the adoption of a broad-based approach while others may not. Consequently, adoption of that approach leaves a corporation open to the risk that it will experience some increase in its cost of capital.

Unfortunately, these conclusions must be qualified further in order to make them realistic. The model from which they were derived rested on the simplifying but unrealizable assumption of complete diversification. It assumed, in other words, that all stockholders held all stocks in the same proportions, although not in the same amounts. This assumption must now be given up. Transactions and information costs, as well as the existence of closely-held corporations, all act to reduce the incentive and ability of risk-averse investors to diversify. Yet some degree of diversification is sought and achieved by the typical investor. The final test is then to assess the significance of limited portfolio diversification for corporate policy with respect to the evaluation of returns on investment opportunities.

With respect to the adoption of an intermediate-based approach to the evaluation of returns, there is a perfect analog in the present situation to the conclusion reached under complete diversification. With less than complete diversification an individual stockholder should require, at a minimum, that each of his corporations include returns appropriable by all of the other corporations whose stock he holds in evaluating returns to investment. The obvious difficulty raised by this proposition in practice is that, since stockholders hold less than completely diversified portfolios, all the stockholders in a corporation will certainly have different equity portfolios. Each stockholder would thus have each corporation whose stock he owns use a different basis for the evaluation of returns to investment. In the face of this confusion, there are only two workable alternatives that corporate managers can adopt. They can ignore all returns not appropriable by their own firm or they can include all returns appropriable within the corporate sector. Adoption of the first ensures that all stockholders forego some returns, while adoption of the second tends to generate additional but unequal returns for all.

Adoption of the intermediate-based approach by all firms nevertheless seems the more desirable policy for stockholders. Given the portfolio of a stockholder, there is, of course, no guarantee that adoption of the intermediate-based approach is the best of all conceivable alternatives. But between the two feasible alternatives, adoption of this approach is likely to produce greater returns for the typical stockholder than would be produced by universal adoption of a narrow-based approach.

There is, however, no assurance that all firms will adopt the intermediate-based approach. Just as in the earlier analysis, the possible existence of maverick corporations must be admitted. On the average, mavericks would have higher returns on their investment. As in the earlier analysis, this would cause their stocks to be pushed up until their risk and return properties, including their correlation with other stocks, made them no more attractive than others. The cost of capital for mavericks would decline, and in the long run these firms would have an opportunity of outcompeting the socially involved corporations. In contrast, however, to the earlier analysis, where complete diversification was assumed, in the present model it is possible for an investor to own only one or a few stocks. What are the implications?

Some investors might own only mavericks. They would not do so because of the superior return the maverick has on its assets; as noted, the market competes away this advantage by raising the price of maverick stock. But some investors might for other reasons own only mavericks, or only one of them, unless they could convince themselves that the gains of diversification outweigh the costs.

The gains an investor can obtain from greater diversification depend (1) on his degree of risk aversion and (2) on the correlation of the returns on his existing holdings with other stocks. On the first, little of a general nature can be said except that the ownership of mavericks, limiting as it does the scope for diversification, will become concentrated among investors with low-risk aversion. If these are few, most investors will own stock also in firms that engage in social expenditures and therefore will have a motive to ask their maverick firms to do likewise in order to benefit their other holdings.

As regards correlation of the maverick with other stocks, algebraically low correlation will reduce the need for diversification. A small number of relatively uncorrelated stocks produces as much diversification as a larger number of more highly correlated. Owners of mavericks with low correlation will have less reasons than others, everything else equal, to diversify into socially-involved corporations. They will have less motive, therefore, to press their maverick firms to become socially involved in order to benefit their other investments.

However, mavericks with low correlation are not likely to be firms belonging to a well-defined homogenous industry. If other stocks are not good substitutes for them, they are likely to operate to some extent in different markets. To the extent that this is true, mavericks will have less opportunity to outcompete, or demonstratively to outperform, socially-involved firms on the basis of their lower cost of capital. This reduces the probability that such mavericks will discourage social expenditures on the part of others.

For mavericks that are highly correlated with other stocks, the last point will not apply. They are likely to be able to outcompete and outperform, and may thus discourage social expenditures. But by virtue of high correlation, they will induce their owners to diversify more extensively. The owners will thus have more motive to press their mavericks for social expenditures.

On the whole, the maverick state is an unstable one for a corporation. Only if the holders of a corporation's stock hold no other stocks does continuation of the maverick state coincide with the interests of stockholders. Since single-stock equity portfolios are uncommon, to say the least, maverick corporations are destined in practice eventually to lose that status.

Thus, even if investors do not hold completely diversified equity portfolios, adoption of an intermediate-based approach to the evaluation of returns from investment is consistent with stockholder interest. Furthermore, although corporations that fail to adopt this approach might enjoy some initial advantage in capital cost, this advantage would be eliminated as their stockholders compelled management to broaden the basis employed for the evaluation of returns.

Adoption of the broader-based approach, which would have corporations include nonmarket returns as well as market returns in evaluating investment opportunities, raises essentially the same problems when investors hold less than completely diversified equity portfolios as when they do hold completely diversified portfolios. The only apparent difference in these situations is that when stockholders hold less than complete portfolios it may seem that they have an interest in disguising their true preferences for nonmarket returns. That is, it may seem that a stockholder who expected to benefit from the adoption of the broader-based approach would, nevertheless, have the corporations whose stock he owns refrain from adopting the broader approach in hopes that those corporations not represented in his portfolio would adopt the approach and thereby provide him nonmarket returns at no cost. But such a strategy by stockholders who expect to benefit is irrational in this case just as it was in the simpler case because it will result in all corporations refraining from adoption of the broad-based approach and the production of lower nonmarket returns than these stockholders find desirable.

Public Policies to Promote Corporate Involvement

The conclusion of this analysis is that the proposition that corporate involvement in social policy is contrary to the stockholders' interest is both misleading and irrelevant. Involvement in social policy is tantamount to the adoption of a policy of evaluating investment opportunities by including returns other than those directly accruing to the investing corporation in the form of increased profit. Once it is recognized that corporations are not usually owned by a group of investors who own shares in only one corporation, but by individuals who as a group typically own shares in a very large number of corporations, the whole concept of stockholder interest becomes extremely fuzzy. Nevertheless, it can be said that the adoption of a policy of including all returns appropriable through the market system will enable investors to reach higher welfare levels than they would if corporations adhered to a narrower approach to evaluation of returns.

Adoption of an even broader approach that included nonmarket returns would be likely to benefit some stockholders and not others, so it is impossible to say whether such a policy is or is not in the stockholders' interest. What can be said is that if there are stockholders who feel their interests would not be served by the adoption of such a policy, then corporations adopting it can expect to experience some increase in their cost of equity capital. The magnitude of this change will depend upon the policies adopted by other corporations, the degree of correlation of returns between adopting and nonadopting corporations, and the proportion of a corporation's stock held by investors who expected to lose from adoption of the broad-based approach.

The preceding analysis assumes that stockholders will instruct their corporate managements to take into account the welfare of other firms, including their own competitors. Since this could be regarded as raising antitrust problems, it becomes important to demonstrate the compatibility of this behavior with the antitrust laws.

Action in restraint of trade, practiced by members of an industry, implies action to benefit competitors. The action also, however, benefits the firm practicing the restraint, and is undertaken for that purpose. Action designed to benefit other firms by creating externalities appropriable through the market is not of that kind. Even though it also benefits the acting firm, the cost by assumption exceeds the benefits to that sole firm. Expenditures that have a positive payoff to the firm must be assumed to be made in any event and are not at issue here. Stockholder pressure on corporations to bring their social spending in line with that of others does not *prima facie* imply restraint of trade.

Antitrust issues might nevertheless be raised if the primary emphasis in this interaction among firms were placed, not on the generation of externalities appropriable by others, but on avoiding the intensified competition from the maverick firm. It is one thing for a stockholder in socially-involved firms A and B and in maverick C to tell C that he ought to engage in training of hardcore unemployed. It may be something else when the managements of A and B try to prevail on C to do so with the objective of blunting C's competitiveness.

The critical point here is the role of the diversified stockholder. A diversified stockholder would have an interest in "encouraging" his firms to conspire to raise prices, just as he has an interest in his firm's engaging in social expenditures. But he would have an interest in a conspiracy to raise prices even if he owned stock in only one of the firms. He has no interest, in that case, in encouraging social expenditures.

Showing that a role in social policy is not inconsistent with stockholder welfare removes one stumbling block to the active participation by corporations in social policy. Nevertheless, the decision to become socially involved may expose a corporation to the risk of adverse shifts in its cost of capital. This raises two questions, namely, (1) what might be done to encourage corporate participation and (2) what should be done.

One obvious means by which corporations might be encouraged to devote a greater proportion of their resources to activities with high social but low private returns is to encourage cooperative decision-making among them to determine the extent of their individual social involvement. To be sure, joint determination among voluntary participants, without the right or ability to enforce a uniform policy, cannot ensure the absence of recalcitrant firms and therefore cannot provide perfect immunity from adverse effect on the costs of capital to socially-involved corporations. Yet cooperative decision-making, particularly among firms whose returns are highly correlated and therefore probably in the same industry, should help to reduce the risks involved.

Though promoting this kind of cooperative decision making—especially among firms in the same industry—immediately appears to conflict with the goals of antitrust policy, the extent of the conflict can easily be overemphasized.

The antitrust laws have not been interpreted by the courts as prohibiting all forms of cooperative behavior among business firms, only that cooperative behavior tends to restrain trade among them. The distinction is best illustrated by the development of the legal status of trade associations under Section 1 of the Sherman Act. Although trade associations are obviously instruments for promoting and facilitating cooperative behavior through the collection and exchange of information and the discussion of problems common to the members, such associations are not in themselves illegal. On the other hand, to preserve their good standing at law, trade associations must avoid activities which may lead to or greatly facilitate cooperative determination of price, output, or investment policies. In addition, they must be sure not to adopt policies that disadvantage would-be entrants into the markets served by their members.

Thus, although assessment of potential antitrust liability is a hazardous occupation, it seems a reasonable guess that there would be considerable room for cooperation by corporations in determining the extent of their social involvement, without incurring risks of antitrust litigation. Nevertheless, the degree of cooperation that could be effected within the present legal boundaries is undoubtedly insufficient to eliminate completely the risks associated with assuming an active role in social policy.

Whether it would be wise to relax the vigor of antitrust enforcement as a means of stimulating social activities in the private sector is very much a matter of opinion. There is certainly room for an expanded role for corporations in social policy. But governments will continue to play a major role in formulating social goals and no less in executing and financing specific programs. In carrying out these functions, governments will frequently wish to procure products and services from the private sector and at times may find it advantageous to contract with firms to execute major social programs or program elements. Past government procurement experience in other areas indicates that the preservation of a competitive procurement environment should be a primary policy objective.

In particular, procurement of social-program elements may raise many problems similar to those encountered in weapons-system procurement. For example, social programs may often call for the production of goods or the rendering of services whose performance characteristics or desired quality can, at best, be only vaguely specified or measured. For this as well as other reasons, project costs and completion times may be typically subject to high degrees of uncertainty. Attempts to deal with this uncertainty in weapons-system procurements have led to the evolution of a multitude of contractual forms designed to allocate the risks in some equitable fashion between the government and its suppliers. Yet all of these contractual forms leave room for inefficiency through overstatement of target costs unless contracts are let competitively.

Adoption of a permissive attitude toward cooperation with respect to social involvement by corporations seems to carry with it a danger that competition in the supply of goods and services required for social programs might be impaired. This could in turn lead to inefficiencies and higher costs for certain social programs that makes a relaxation of antitrust vigilance of questionable value as an instrument for the promotion of corporate participation in social policy.

Notes

Chapter 1. Corporate Philanthropy (pages 3–19)

[1]John H. Watson, III, reports that resolutions designed to restrict corporate giving generally draw no more than 5 per cent of the shares voted. In the years investigated by Watson, all such resolutions were defeated. See his "Corporate Contributions Policy," *The Conference Board Record*, Vol. IV, No. 6 (June 1967), p. 13.

[2]It is interesting that this measure seems to have been opposed by President Roosevelt, who was, however, persuaded by those engaged in philanthropic work to refrain from vetoing the act.

[3]These figures are derived from U.S. Internal Revenue Service, *Statistics of Income: Corporation Income Tax Returns* (Washington, D.C.: U.S. Government Printing Office, various years).

[4]William J. Baumol and William G. Bowen, *Performing Arts—The Economic Dilemma* (New York: Twentieth Century Fund, 1966), chapters 13-14.

[5]It should be noted that Watson's work and, in particular, his careful surveys are the most illuminating and reliable source of information on corporate contributions, their magnitude, their trends, their distribution, and the amounts coming from firms of different types. Some of the most thoughtful work on the rationale of corporate contribution has been contributed by Professor Richard Eells. For a recent discussion see his "A Philosophy for Corporate Giving," *The Conference Board Record*, Vol. V, No. 1 (January 1968), pp. 14-18.

[6]It has been pointed out by Eells, *op. cit.* (note 5), p. 15, that the figures omit such contributions as gifts-in-kind, the lending of company personnel and good will expenditures for local causes. He notes that while business contributions amount to about 6 per cent of total private philanthropy, if religious causes are omitted, corporate giving jumps to perhaps one-fourth or even one-third of the total.

[7]John H. Watson, III, *Report on Company Contributions for 1968* (New York: National Industrial Conference Board, 1969), p. 6.

[8]American Society of Corporate Secretaries, *Corporate Contributions Report*, 3rd ed. (New York: March 1965).

[9]"139 Companies Report on Corporate Philanthropy," *Business Management* (December 1965), pp. 14-20.

Chapter 2. The Influence of Social Research (pages 20–38)

[1]The following summarize findings from a number of these studies. Bibliographies listing all the separate studies are available from the Institute for Social Research at the University of Michigan.

David G. Bowers, ed., *Applying Modern Management Principles to Sales Organizations* (Ann Arbor: Foundation for Research on Human Behavior, 1963).

David G. Bowers, "Organizational Control in an Insurance Company," *Sociometry*, Vol. 27, No. 2 (June 1964), pp. 230-244.

Dorwin Cartwright and Alvin F. Zander, eds., *Group Dynamics: Research and Theory*, 3rd ed. (New York: Harper, 1968).

Basil Georgopoulos and Floyd C. Mann, *The Community General Hospital* (New York: Macmillan, 1962).

Robert L. Kahn, "Human Relations on the Shop Floor," in Edward M. Hugh-Jones, ed., *Human Relations and Modern Management* (Amsterdam: North Holland Publishing Co., 1958), pp. 43-74.

Robert L. Kahn and others, *Organizational Stress: Studies in Role Conflict and Ambiguity* (New York: Wiley, 1964).

Daniel Katz and Robert L. Kahn, *The Social Psychology of Organizations* (New York: Wiley, 1966).

Daniel Katz and Robert L. Kahn, "Some Recent Findings in Human Relations Research," in Society for the Psychological Study of Social Issues, *Readings in Social Psychology* (New York: Holt, 1952), pp. 650-665.

Rensis Likert, *The Human Organization: Its Management and Value* (New York: McGraw-Hill, 1967).

Rensis Likert, *New Patterns of Management* (New York: McGraw-Hill, 1961).

Rensis Likert, "The Relationship Between Management Behavior and Social Structure—Improving Human Performance: Better Theory, More Accurate Accounting," in International CIOS Management Congress, 15th, Tokyo, *The New Role of Management: Innovation, Integration and Internationalization; Proceedings* (1969), pp. 136-146.

Rensis Likert and David G. Bowers, "Organizational Theory and Human Resource Accounting," *American Psychologist*, Vol. 24, No. 6 (June 1969), pp. 585-592.

Floyd C. Mann and Howard J. Baumgartel, *The Supervisor's Concern with Costs in an Electric Power Company* (Ann Arbor: University of Michigan, Institute for Social Research, Survey Research Center, 1953).

Floyd C. Mann and James Dent, *Appraisals of Supervisors and Attitudes of Their Employees in an Electric Power Company* (Ann Arbor: University of Michigan, Institute for Social Research, Survey Research Center, 1954).

Floyd C. Mann and L. Richard Hoffman, *Automation and the Worker: A Study of Social Change in Power Plants* (New York: Holt, 1960).

Floyd C. Mann and Franklin W. Neff, *Managing Major Change in Organizations: An Undeveloped Area of Administration and Social Research* (Ann Arbor: Foundation for Research on Human Behavior, 1961).

Floyd C. Mann and others, *The Productivity of Work Groups* (Ann Arbor: University of Michigan, Institute for Social Research, Survey Research Center, 1963).

Floyd C. Mann and others, "The Supervisor and Absence Rates," *Supervisory Management*, Vol. 2, No. 7 (June 1957), pp. 7-14.

Alfred J. Marrow and others, *Management by Participation: Creating a Climate for Personal and Organizational Development* (New York: Harper, 1967).

Paul E. Mott and others, *Shift Work: The Social, Psychological, and Physical Consequences* (Ann Arbor: University of Michigan Press, 1965).

Donald C. Pelz and Frank M. Andrews, *Scientists in Organizations: Productive Climates for Research and Development* (New York: Wiley, 1966).

Stanley E. Seashore, *Group Cohesiveness in the Industrial Work Group* (Ann Arbor: University of Michigan, Institute for Social Research, Survey Research Center, 1954).

Stanley E. Seashore and David G. Bowers, *Changing the Structure and Functioning of an Organization* (Ann Arbor: University of Michigan, Institute for Social Research, Survey Research Center, 1963).

Stanley E. Seashore and David G. Bowers, "Durability of Organizational Change," *American Psychologist*, Vol. 25, No. 3 (March 1970), pp. 227-233.

Arnold S. Tannenbaum, *Control in Organizations* (New York: McGraw-Hill, 1968).

Arnold S. Tannenbaum, *Social Psychology of the Work Organization* (Belmont: Wadsworth Publishing Co., 1966).

[2]Chris Argyris, *Integrating the Individual and the Organization* (New York: Wiley, 1964).

Edwin A. Fleishman and others, *Leadership and Supervision in Industry: An Evaluation of a Supervisory Training Program* (Columbus: Ohio State University, Bureau of Educational Research, 1955).

Robert H. Guest, *Organizational Change: The Effect of Successful Leadership* (Homewood: Dorsey Press, 1962).

Mason Haire, ed., *Modern Organization Theory*, (New York: Wiley, 1959).

John K. Hemphill, *Group Dimensions: A Manual for Their Measurement* (Columbus: Ohio State University, Bureau of Business Research, 1956).

Stuart M. Klein and R. R. Ritti, "Work Pressure, Supervisory Behavior and Employee Attitudes: A Factor Analysis," *Personnel Psychology*, Vol. 23, No. 2 (Summer 1970), pp. 153-167.

Jyuji Misumi and Sanshiro Shirakashi, "An Experimental Study of the Effects of Supervisory Behavior on Productivity and Morale in a Hierarchical Organization," *Human Relations*, Vol. 19, No. 3 (August 1966), pp. 297-307.

Jyuji Misumi and Toshiaki Tasaki, "A Field Study of the Effectiveness of Supervisory Patterns in a Japanese Hierarchical Organization," *Japanese Journal of Educational Social Psychology*, Vol. 4 (1965) pp. 1-13.

Karlene Roberts and others, "Organizational Leadership Satisfaction and Productivity: A Comparative Analysis," *Academy of Management Journal*, Vol. 11, No. 4 (December 1968), pp. 401-414.

William F. Whyte, ed., *Money and Motivation: An Analysis of Incentives in Industry* (New York: Harper, 1955).

[3]William C. Pyle, "Human Resource Accounting," *Financial Analysts Journal*, Vol. 26, No. 5 (September/October 1970), pp. 69-78.

[4]Rensis Likert, *The Human Organization: Its Management and Value* (New York: McGraw-Hill, 1967), chapter 4.

Rensis Likert, *New Patterns of Management* (New York: McGraw-Hill, 1961), chapter 9.

Arnold S. Tannenbaum, *Control in Organizations* (New York: McGraw-Hill, 1968).

[5]Rensis Likert, *The Human Organization: Its Management and Value*. Copyright © 1967 by McGraw-Hill, pp. 180-182. Used with permission.

Contributors

WILLIAM J. BAUMOL, professor of economics at Princeton University, has taught, written, and consulted in a wide range of economic fields. A native of New York City, Baumol received his undergraduate degree in 1942 from the College of the City of New York. Following wartime service with the War Food Administration and the U.S. Army, he received his doctorate in 1949 at the London School of Economics and joined the Princeton faculty the same year.

Baumol gained nationwide attention as co-author (with William G. Bowen) of *Performing Arts—The Economic Dilemma*, published in 1966 by The Twentieth Century Fund. Among his other published works are *Economic Theory and Operations Analysis; Economic Dynamics, Business Behavior, Value and Growth; Welfare Economics and the Theory of the State;* and *Economic Processes and Policies* (with Lester V. Chandler).

Baumol has been a visiting lecturer at the University of California and elsewhere and has held a Guggenheim Foundation Fellowship. He has been associated with the European Productivity Agency and the British Foundation for Management Education. He is chairman of the faculty salary committee of the American Association of University Professors, and is a past vice president of the American Economic Association.

RENSIS LIKERT has played a leading role in the development of research techniques in the social sciences since the late 1930's. He headed the Division of Program Surveys, which was created to conduct sample interview surveys for the Department of Agriculture and other government agencies, and later served as Director of the Morale Division of the postwar U.S. Strategic Bombing Survey. In 1946, Likert became director of the Survey Research Center (now the Institute for Social Research) at the University of Michigan, which post he held until retiring in 1970. He is now chairman of the board of Rensis Likert Associates.

After finishing his undergraduate work at the University of Michigan, Likert received his doctorate at Columbia University in 1932. His studies in recent years have focused on organizational theory and management practice. His book, *New Patterns of Management*, received several awards, including the American Academy of Management's McKinsey Foundation 1962 Book Award. *The Human Organization: Its Management and Value* appeared in 1967. He is a past president of the American Statistical Association.

HENRY C. WALLICH has combined an academic career with distinguished government service. During the Eisenhower Administration, he was on leave from the economic faculty at Yale University from 1958 to 1959 as Assistant Secretary of the Treasury and from 1959 to 1961 as a member of the Council of Economic Advisers. He currently serves as Senior Consultant to the Secretary of the Treasury.

Wallich was born in Berlin, Germany, studied at Oxford University, and came to this country as a security analyst in the mid-1930's. He left the securities business in 1941 to enter Harvard University, where he received his doctorate in economics in 1944. From 1941 to 1951, he was Chief of the Foreign Research Division of the Federal Reserve Bank of New York. He has been professor of economics at Yale since 1951, and in 1970 was appointed Seymour H. Knox Professor of Economics.

His books include *Monetary Problems of an Export Economy; Mainsprings of the German Revival;* and *The Cost of Freedom*. He has also been an editorial contributor to the *Washington Post* and is presently a columnist for *Newsweek*.

JOHN J. MCGOWAN, associate professor of economics at Yale University, has given his attention to government regulatory policy in the fields of communications and business mergers.

After completing his undergraduate work at the University of Toronto in 1958, McGowan pursued his graduate studies in economics at Yale, receiving his doctorate in 1965. He has been a participant in Brookings Institution conferences on the Use and Regulation of the Radio Spectrum and on Technological Change in the Regulated Industries. He has also been a discussant in a Session on the Theory of the Firm held by the Econometric Society.

His writings include "The Effects of Alternative Antimerger Policies on the Size Distribution of Firms," *Yale Economic Essays;* "Vertical Integration in Cement" (with M. J. Peck), *The Antitrust Bulletin*, and "Competition, Regulation, and Performance in Television Broadcasting," *Washington University Law Quarterly*.

Index

Accounting procedures
  and balance sheet, 28-31
  for evaluating goodwill and human resources, 21-24, 29-30, 31, 37-38
Advertising, 10
Air pollution control
  government role in, 20
  as public good, 12-13
  and stockholder interest, 41, 47
American Association of Fund-Raising Counsel, Inc., 7n
Antitrust laws, and social expenditures, 56-59
Arts
  business control of, 4
  and corporate giving, 8-10
  growth of costs in, 11
Assets
  human resources as, 21
  liquidation of, 24
  physical, worth of, 23

Balance sheet, misleading aspects of, 28-31
Banks, 8
  loyalty to firms of, 21, 31
Barry, R. G., Corporation, 31
Bequests, 6
Bonuses, 24
Book value, 24
Business organizations
  communication in, 26, 29, 32, 33-34
  control of arts by, 4
  and corporate philanthropy, 3-19
  and goodwill, 21, 23, 24, 30, 31, 33, 38
  human resources of, 21, 22-32
  interaction-influence process in, 26, 33-34
  leadership processes used in, 26
  payroll-earning ratio in, 21
  publics of, 31-33, 37-38
  reaction to goals in, 27
  role of subordinates in, 26, 27
  social expenditures by, 45, 53, 54, 56, 59
  and stockholder welfare, 39-59
  teamwork in, 27
  see also Corporations

Capital
  cost of, 46, 49-50, 52
  sources of, 33
Cash balance, 28, 31
Cities, investments in, 4
Civic causes, 9
Communication, in firms, 26, 29, 32
  and policy, 33
Community loyalty, 21, 30, 31
Company foundations, 18-19
Consortia, 14-15, 17, 18
Corporate philanthropy
  arguments against, 3-4
  background of, 5-10
  from 1936 to 1969, 7
  and government policy, 5
  performance of, evaluated, 10-18 *passim*
  and public goods, 11-18
  as sanctioned by courts, 4, 6-8, 40
  and self-interest, 11-18 *passim*
  and tax benefits, 5
  undertaking activities in, 18-19
  volume of, 5-6, 7, 8, 15-19
Corporate responsibility
  and investor, 3-4, 17-18, 39-59
  and social research, 20-38
Corporate sector, return appropriable by, 41, 43, 44, 46, 47, 48, 50, 52, 55

67

INDEX

Corporations
  maverick, 45-46, 52-54
  contribution procedures in, 18-19
  cost of capital for, 46, 49-50, 52
  generosity of, 10-11
  government control of, 20-21, 31, 32, 38
  involvement of, in social policy, 39-59
  and profits, 42-43
  and public goods, 11-14, 41, 47
  size of, 10, 11
  social responsibility of, 18, 20-38 *passim*
  see also Business organizations
Cost reduction, and shift in management system, 28-32, 38
Costs
  of capital, 46, 49-50, 52, 53, 54, 55, 57
  of social involvement, 45, 53, 54, 56, 59
  transaction and information, 51
Cost-sharing agreements, 15
Cultural activities
  dollar contributions to, 9
  rationale for giving to, 8-10
Customer loyalty, 21, 23
  dollar estimates of, 31
  liquidation of, 30
Customers, communication with, 33

Decision-making
  group model of, 35, 36-37
  man-to-man model of, 34, 35
  and science-based management systems, 21-37 *passim*
Departments, productivity of, 25-38

Earnings, 23
  and liquidation of valuable assets, 24, 28-32
  and management systems, 24-32
Education
  dependence upon business of, 4
  dollar contributions to, 9
  gifts to, 4, 8, 15, 40
  higher, 9, 11, 16-17, 40
  increase in costs of, 11
  secondary, 9, 11
Excess profits tax, 5
"Excludability property," 12-13, 14-16
External benefits, 13, 14, 17, 56; *see also* Nonmarket returns

Fellowships, 9
Financial reports, 24, 28

Foundations, 18-19
Free enterprise system, 11

Ghettos, and corporate giving, 4
Goals, reaction to, 27, 29, 32
Goodwill, 21
  computing value of, 23, 24
  and decision-making, 33
  dollar estimates of, 31
  liquidation of, 30
Government
  and corporate philanthropy, 5
  demand for controls by, 20-21, 31, 32, 38
Gross national product, 6

Health and welfare
  dollar contributions to, 9
  gifts related to, 8
  and government control, 20
  increase in costs in, 11
Hierarchical pressure, 29
Hospitals, gifts to, 8, 9
Housing, 4
Human Organization, The: Its Management and Value (Likert), $27n$, $35n$
Human resources
  computing value of, 21, 22-24, 29-30, 31, 37-38
  dollar estimates of, 31, 38
  vs. earnings and productivity, 24-32
  liquidation of, 28-31
  and shifts in management systems, 28-30

Industrial waste, 20
Industry organizations, 17
Inflation, 11
Institute for Social Research, 24, 31
Interaction-influence process, in firms, 26, 33
  man-to-man model in, 34, 35
Internal Revenue Code, 1935, amendment of, 5, 10
Investments
  broad-based approach to, 46-50
  diversified, 39, 43-46, 50-55
  maverick, 45, 52-54, 56
  narrow-based, 43-44
  and nonmarket returns, 46-50, 54
  in public goods, 11-18, 47
  and returns appropriable by corporate sector, 41, 43, 44, 46-48, 50
  in single companies, 39, 54
  see also Stockholders

Labor force, 44
Labor relations, 29, 30
Leadership processes, 26

Management
 levels of, 33
 rewards for, based on short-term gains, 24
 social concern of, 6, 16
 and social research, 21-37 *passim*
Management systems
 comparisons of, 25-37 *passim*
 effects of shifts in, 28-30
 and human resources, 21-24, 28-30
 science-based, 21-37 *passim*
 table comparing, 26-37
 "win-lose" battling in, 34
Market forces, 39, 40
Marketing department, 34
Market share, 30
Maverick corporations
 cost of capital for, 52, 53
 vs. socially involved corporations, 45-46, 52-54, 56
 social pressure on, 45
Medical costs, 11
Military-industrial complex, 4
Motivation, in firms, 29, 32

National Banking Act, 8
National defense, 13
National Industrial Conference Board (NICB), 9n, 10, 11n
Nonmarket returns, 46-50, 54
Nonprofit organizations, 16
 growing financial needs of, 11

Oil exploration, joint exploration of, as model, 14-15
Organizations. *See* Business organizations; Corporations

Payroll-to-earnings ratio, 23
Performing arts
 gifts to, 9, 17
 increased costs in, 11
Personnel department, 33
Personnel reductions, 28
Personnel training
 and gifts to schools, 4, 8, 15-16
 marginal benefits of, 41
Philanthropy, private, 6; *see also* Corporate philanthropy
Pollution control, 12-13, 20, 41, 47
Portfolio diversification, 39, 43-46, 50-55
Price-raising, and antitrust laws, 56-57, 58

Princeton University, 6-8
Productivity, and management systems, 25-32
Profits
 and management systems, 25-32
 maximization of, and social policy, 42-43
 see also Returns, appropriable
Profit system, 12
Promotions, 24
Public goods
 and corporate philanthropy, 15-18
 illustration of, 14-15
 and self-interest, 11-14, 41, 47
Purchasing department, 33

Recreation projects, 16
Religious causes, gifts to, 9
Research grants, 9
Returns, appropriable
 by corporate sector, 41, 43, 44, 46-48, 50, 52, 55
 degrees of, 40-43
 vs. nonmarket returns, 46-50, 54

Sales department, 33
Scholarships, 9
Services, public, 11-14; *see also* Public goods
Shares, and firm's total value, 24; *see also* Investments
Sherman Act, 57
Smith, A. P., v. Barlow (1953), 6-8, 40
Social expenditure. *See* Costs
Social research
 and corporate responsibility, 20-38 *passim*
 impact of, 37-38
Social responsibility, 16
 in corporate management, 20-38
 corporate role in, 39-59
 and corporate self-interest, 11-18, 43-46
 and philanthropic programs, 3-19
Stockholder groups, pressures from, 4
Stockholders
 diversified, 39, 43-46, 50-55
 explanations to, 17-18
 loyalty of, 21, 30, 31
 opposition of, to corporate philanthropy, 3-4
 and profit maximization, 42-43
 representation of interests of, 24, 33-34, 39-59 *passim*; *see*

Stockholders *(continued)*
　　also Stockholder welfare
　risk averse, 43-44, 50-51, 53

　satisfaction in social benefits
　　by, 47
　see also Investments
Stockholder welfare
　broad-based approach to, 46-50
　and corporate social involvement,
　　39-59 *passim*
　and limited diversification,
　　50-55
　and portfolio diversification,
　　43-46
　and profits, 40-43
Suppliers
　communication with, 33
　loyalty of, 21, 30, 31
Symphony orchestras, gifts to,
　10, 16

Taxation, tax rates
　and company foundations, 18-19
　and public goods, 13
Tax benefits, 5, 6, 10
Total value, of business firm
　vs. book value, 24
　computation of, 24
Trade organizations, 17
　and antitrust law, 57-58
Treasurer, company, 33

Unions, 33
United funds, gifts to, 8, 9

Voluntary groups, 14-15

Water pollution, 20, 47
Watson, John H., 9*n,* 10, 11*n*
Work measurement, 28-29

About CED...

The Committee for Economic Development (CED) is an independent research and educational organization of 200 leading businessmen and educators. With the help of advisory boards of distinguished economists and social scientists, CED trustees conduct research and formulate policy recommendations in four major areas of public policy: (1) the national economy, (2) the international economy, (3) education and urban development, and (4) the management of federal, state, and local government.

CED is nonprofit, nonpartisan, and nonpolitical. It is supported largely by contributions from business, foundations, and individuals. CED's objective is to promote stable growth with rising living standards and increasing opportunities for all Americans.

The Committee for Economic Development draws its 200 trustees largely from the ranks of board chairmen and presidents of business corporations and financial institutions, and from the ranks of university presidents. These trustees are chosen for their individual capacities, for their understanding of public problems, and for their willingness to view these problems from the standpoint of the general welfare and not from that of any special interest group.

All CED policy recommendations must be approved by a fifty-man group of trustees, the Research and Policy Committee, which alone can speak for the organization. These recommendations are set forth in Statements on National Policy and are the result of months of research, discussion, and policy formulation.

In connection with the publication of a statement, CED often publishes documents originally prepared by scholars as background papers but deemed worthy of wider circulation, as in the case of the present Supplementary Paper. Though publication of such papers must be authorized by an editorial board of trustees and academic advisors as a contribution to knowledge, the opinions and conclusions expressed are solely those of the individual authors and do not reflect the policies or views of the trustees.